Clergy and Laity Burnout

Creative Leadership Series

Assimilating New Members, Lyle E. Schaller
Beginning a New Pastorate, Robert G. Kemper
The Care and Feeding of Volunteers, Douglas W. Johnson
Creative Stewardship, Richard B. Cunningham
Time Management, Speed B. Leas
Your Church Can Be Healthy, C. Peter Wagner
Leading Churches Through Change, Douglas Alan Walrath
Building an Effective Youth Ministry, Glenn E. Ludwig
Preaching and Worship in the Small Church,
William Willimon and Robert L. Wilson
Church Growth, Donald McGavran and George G. Hunter III
The Pastor's Wife Today, Donna Sinclair
The Small Town Church, Peter J. Surrey
Strengthening the Adult Sunday School Class, Dick Murray
Church Advertising, Steve Dunkin
Women as Pastors, edited by Lyle E. Schaller
Leadership and Conflict, Speed B. Leas
Church Finance in a Complex Economy, Manfred Holck, Jr.
The Tithe, Douglas W. Johnson
Surviving Difficult Church Members, Robert D. Dale
Your Church Has Personality, Kent R. Hunter
The Word on Families, G. William Sheek
Five Audiences, Warren J. Hartman
How to Build a Magnetic Church, Herb Miller
Teaching the Bible to Adults and Youth, Dick Murray
Keys to Building Youth Ministry, Glenn E. Ludwig
The Rural Church, Edward W. Hassinger,
John S. Holik, and J. Kenneth Benson
Clergy and Laity Burnout, William H. Willimon

Clergy and Laity Burnout

William H. Willimon

Creative Leadership Series
Lyle E. Schaller

Abingdon Press / Nashville

CLERGY AND LAITY BURNOUT

Copyright © 1989 by Abingdon Press

This book is printed on acid-free paper.

Library of Congress Cataloging-in-Publication Data

Willimon, William H.
  Clergy and laity burnout / William H. Willimon.
    p. cm. — (Creative leadership series)
  ISBN 0-687-08655-8 (alk. paper : pbk.)
  1. Clergy—Psychology. 2. Church officers—Psychology.
3. Clergy—Job stress. 4. Church officers—Job stress. 5. Burn out
(Psychology) I. Title. II. Series.
BV4398.W55 1988   88-22649
253'.2—dc19   CIP

Scripture quotations in this publication are from the Revised Standard
Version of the Bible, copyrighted 1946, 1952, © 1971, 1973 by the Division of
Christian Education of the National Council of the churches of Christ in the
U.S.A., and are used by permission.

MANUFACTURED BY THE PARTHENON PRESS AT
NASHVILLE, TENNESSEE, UNITED STATES OF AMERICA

FOREWORD

"Our pastor told us he was 'burned out' and needed a sabbatical, so we gave him a six-week leave of absence in addition to his regular vacation," explained a leader of a county-seat church. "That was nearly three years ago. He came back from that sabbatical all charged up and raring to go. It was obvious to all of us that he needed and deserved that leave of absence, and it was clear we had done the right thing. This past Sunday, he announced from the pulpit that he was burned out and was planning to leave the ministry for a secular job. Sunday after next will be his last Sunday here with us. Some of us feel guilty that we have failed our pastor. Did we not do something we should have? After all, he's only forty-six years old, and he could have spent another twenty years in the ministry. I hate to see someone who's been called by God give up the ministry after having all that training. What's your advice?"

"My third- and fourth-grade Sunday school teacher came in to see me last Tuesday," complained a minister one day in February. "She told me she was burned out and that she was quitting at the end of the month. I've found someone to take her place until the end of the year, but that's not the problem. Why would Martha, who's in very good health and who has taught that same class in the same room for nine years, suddenly decide to give it up in the middle of the year? When I came here three years ago, she told me, 'Reverend, as far as I'm concerned, you can make any and all the changes you want around here with one exception. That exception is that I want to continue to teach the third- and fourth-grade Sunday school class. That's my way of showing how I love the Lord. Don't try to take it away from me.' As far as I could tell, she was doing an excellent job, and I was delighted that she loved to do it. Now, all of a sudden, she tells me she's a victim of burnout and wants to quit. How do I go about ministering to her?''

"I can't understand why my wife doesn't burn out," declared an anxious husband and father who also was one of four insurance agents in a town fewer than six hundred residents. "She's the pastor of a church here in town, and she also serves another little congregation that meets in a building out in the country, nine miles north of here. We have two kids; one's two-and-a-half years old, and the other one is in kindergarten. Last week the doctor told her she's pregnant again, and she is delighted. I help as much as I can with the kids, but my work means that I have to spend many evenings out calling on my clients. You can't build up an insurance business sitting in an office all day. We do have access to two good babysitters, but there's a limit to what they can do. When I tell my wife she's the number one candidate for burnout in this county, she just laughs at me. The people at both churches love her, and I've been told dozens of times that she's the best minister they've had in more than forty years. I think she's a superb preacher. She really loves people. She's also an excellent administrator, and she knows how to manage her time. But she is overextended. She's trying to crowd thirty-six hours of work into every day. Sometimes I think I ought to cut back on my work and become the homemaker in our family, but there's no way we could live on the salary she makes. What keeps her going?"

The simplest response to these questions asked above is: "Read Will Willimon's book on burnout."

This book speaks to the lay leader who is deeply disturbed by the pastor's decision to leave the professional ministry. It explains why an extended leave of absence may be appropriate treatment for burnout, but that it may not be a cure. This book will help the lay leader understand why some ministers complain about burnout, and it will help both the clergy and the laity accept the fact that leaving the pastoral ministry may be both an appropriate and an honorable course of action.

This book, if it had been available, might have been useful to the minister in our first quotation above to read while on sabbatical. It could have transformed his understanding of the pastoral ministry and of his role in it. The combination of a sabbatical and this book could have enabled him to see that the dissipation of commitment, the loss of energy, and self doubt have been a normal part of the pilgrimage of many called by God. This book, plus the time for reflection provided by a sabbatical, might have provided the opportunity for that pastor to shift from a reactive approach to ministry to an initiating leadership role. It also must be recognized that the combination of sabbatical time for personal reflection plus this book might have caused that pastor to return and declare, "Friends, I've discovered that I am not cut out for this expression of my Christian commitment, and in another month I expect to be in secular employment." What took this minister nearly three years to work through might have been compressed into three months—which might have reduced the extent of the self-induced guilt among the laity in that congregation.

This book also provides useful clues to the minister who is disturbed by the unexpected decision of a Sunday school teacher to give up a responsibility she had been carrying, and apparently enjoying, for nine years. It can help both the laity and the clergy understand the causes of what is popularly labeled "burnout," and it also offers some wise and informed counsel on responses to that affliction.

Perhaps the one who will gain the most from reading this book is the spouse of that overworked, overburdened, and overextended pastor. Dr. Willimon makes it clear that hard and productive work rarely is a cause of burnout. This insurance agent's pregnant wife clearly is a hardworking individual in a high stress setting. That does not necessarily mean that she is a candidate for burnout. It appears that the combination of commitment, affirmation, and, perhaps most influential of all, a sense of meaning in what she is doing greatly reduce the chance that this very busy minister-wife-mother will suffer from burnout. She may, if she gives birth to another three or four children, see the value of a live-in homemaker who can help with the housework. But as long as the flame of commitment is fed by a feeling of self-worth and a conviction that there is meaning in the combined role of pastor-wife-mother, it is unlikely that she will become a candidate for burnout.

This is one of many books in THE CREATIVE LEADERSHIP SERIES, written for both laity and clergy as they seek to understand more clearly God's call to the people of the churches and to be faithful and obedient in responding to the call of their Lord.

Lyle E. Schaller
Yokefellow Institute
Richmond, Indiana

Contents

What have we our time and strength for, but to lay them out for God? What is a candle made for but to burn? Burned and wasted we must be; but is it not fitter it should be in lighting men to heaven and in working for God than in living to the flesh?

Richard Baxter, *The Reformed Pastor*, 1655

INTRODUCTION:

MOSES—FRUSTRATION AND FULFILLMENT

As Jesus once observed, some who put their hand to the plow look back (Luke 9:62). Discipleship is no different from any venture that requires perseverance, tenacity, courage, fear, and persistence. Some who begin such ventures fall away. In this book, we will explore factors that contribute to a dissipation of commitment among laypeople and their clergy in the church.

To begin this exploration, the first statement that needs to be made is that dissipation, loss of energy, "burnout," and flagging commitment *are normal and expected aspects of the Christian life.* Scripture is full of accounts of persons who, having put their hands to the plow and launched out on some great venture for God, have faltered. Moses is only one example.

Moses steps onto the stage of the Exodus narrative as a man who is chosen for the task of leading the Israelites out of Egyptian bondage. From the beginning, Moses feels that he is ill equipped for so great a task. "Who am I that I should go to Pharaoh, and bring the sons of

Israel out of Egypt?" God responds to Moses' self-doubts by promising Moses that a Divine presence will strengthen him to execute the Divine commission. Powered by the promise of God to be with him, Moses begins his task. The people of Israel join with Moses, moving out of slavery, responding to their faith that "the Lord had visited the people of Israel and that he had seen their affliction."

But a promise of Divine assistance does not always result in instant success. Exodus 5 shows the Pharaoh responding to Moses' words with insolence: "Who is the Lord, that I should heed his voice and let Israel go? I do not know the Lord and moreover I will not let Israel go" (Exod. 5:3). Moses and Aaron continue negotiations, even offering a compromise of a three-day journey into the wilderness instead of a complete Exodus. Pharaoh refuses to let the people go even for a short period. In fact, the Pharoah responds by increasing the work load of the Hebrew slaves (Exod. 5:10-14).

Moses' effort to win the freedom of Israel has ended in failure, and this failure leads to even greater oppression. For their efforts to liberate the people from slavery, Moses and Aaron are rewarded by becoming the subjects of a law suit brought against them by the people (5:20-21)! The oppressed people, who were to be liberated, have turned on their liberators. In fact, Moses and Aaron are charged with actions that could lead to the death of the Hebrews.

In despair, Moses responds to the people's rejection of his leadership by rejecting God. "Then Moses turned again to the Lord and said, 'Oh Lord, why hast thou done evil to this people? Why didst thou ever send me?' " (Exod. 5:22). Crisis in Moses' ability to lead the people has resulted in a crisis in his own faith. Moses not only feels like a failure himself but also accuses God of failure.

Scholars believe that Exodus 5 contains the earliest stratum of the Exodus tradition, the earliest narrative of negotiation and failure, which was later expanded in Exodus 7–12. It is a picture of unremitting frustration, despair, and failure. With each successive plague, Moses and the people learn just how difficult liberation from Egyptian slavery will be.

This narrative also gives us a picture of Moses' (and especially God's) resourcefulness in the face of repeated failure. The plagues start out as rather minor catastrophes. But each time Pharaoh refuses to let the people go, the intensity, seriousness, and catastrophic qualities of the plagues increase. Thus the narrator is able to show us that God is infinitely resourceful and persistent and that God's leaders, such as Moses, ought to be so as well. (See Aaron Wildavsky, *The Nursing Father: Moses As a Political Leader* [Tuscaloosa: The University of Alabama Press, 1984]).

The negotiations cycle ends in Exodus 10 with failure. The story can go no further unless God creates some new possibility. The dramatic new possibility is the Passover event. The interpreter of this event may have difficulty in understanding the violence in the killing of the Egyptian firstborn children. We should remind ourselves that this incident comes only at the end of repeated attempts to win freedom for the Hebrew slaves and after Pharaoh's own infanticide of the

Hebrew children. The theological point behind the narrative is that repeated failures did not ultimately thwart the work of God or God's leader, Moses.

For our purposes, a fascinating aspect of the Exodus narrative is that difficulties with failure and despair are not over when the Hebrews are finally led by Moses out of Egypt. In fact, the difficulties intensify. The difficulties God's people face would be relatively simple if they were always the difficulties of the oppressed suffering under the evil oppressor. We could then assume that the major task of God's people is simply to liberate the oppressed from oppressors like Pharoah. The Bible depicts a much more complicated story than do many of our contemporary theologies. We find that, when the children of Israel finally are free, they are still in the wilderness, still on the way. Out in the wilderness, Moses fails again. It doesn't take long for the people to murmur against Moses and God. They rebel against Moses and threaten to kill him. No sooner has God established a covenant with the people than they worship the golden calf. Under the leadership of Joshua, the people again fall away. And, of course, the biblical story continues with other chosen leaders—Samuel, David, Solomon, and others. The story even continues telling of a new Moses, another Davidic Messiah, who is to bring liberation for the whole world. Still there are failures. Still the people are unable to be completely faithful. The long story of the faithlessness of God's people comes to a climax when, in response to God's greatest leader, the people succeed in doing to him what they had tried to do to Moses—kill him. His body, hanging on a cross outside of Jerusalem, stands as a stark last chapter in an age-old story of the failure of God's people to do God's will.

Recitation of our story reminds us that a sense of failure, a sense of despair at our human inability to live up to our commitments, pervades the story of God's dealings with us. We encounter no apostasy, infidelity, backsliding, or despair in our churches today that has not been encountered among God's people long before us. But, of course, for us Christians, that is not the whole story. Even as God refused to be stumped by the hard-heartedness of Pharoah, even as God refused to turn his back on the infidelity of the Hebrews in the wilderness, so also God refused to let people go even when they crucified his Son. Time and again God has returned to us, renewing us, creating fresh possibilities, opening up our future, refreshing us with his life-giving spirit.

This same tension between hope and despair, failure and victory—tension that is at the heart of the biblical story—continues to be at the heart of church life today. You and I live within the middle of this tension. Some days, we are Moses standing in despair before the bickering, faithless children of Israel. On other days, we are Moses arguing with God, refusing to prophesy, unsure of ourselves and the power of God. There are still other days when we are part of the amazing liberation of God. We are privileged to witness the liberation of people once enslaved. This book is addressed to the living of all of those days. I hope that this book will aid those clergy and laity who struggle to be faithful in ministry.

This study is the result of my own experiences as a

pastor and seminary professor for nearly two decades. Reading and research into the problems of commitment, reflection on scripture, and guided conversations with dozens of pastors and with those who attempt to help pastors and congregations achieve their full potential for ministry have also informed my work. I thank Duke University for the time to do research for and to write this book and to Mrs. Jacquelyn Andrews for her work in preparing the manuscript. I hope that it will be of help in the fulfillment of our vocations to minister in the name of the One who has ministered to each of us.

I

BURNOUT AND
DROPOUT IN CHURCHES:
THE CAUSES

Burnout—the word implies that our energy is gone. We cannot summon the energy to do what needs to be done. We appear distracted, tired, empty. I agree with John A. Sanford's belief (*Ministry Burnout* [New York: Paulist Press, 1982]) that the metaphor of "burnout" is not quite appropriate for the phenomenon among the laity and the clergy we are describing. *Burnout* is a term borrowed from rocketry. It denotes a lack of energy when a rocket, soaring upward, runs out of fuel and falls back to the earth. In one sense, the metaphor may be a bit self-congratulatory. To describe oneself as "burnt out" implies that one is like a brilliant, upward moving rocket that tragically runs out of energy and plunges downward. To say that you are suffering from burnout ignores that you may never have even left the launching pad!

Many of us like to present ourselves as being under constant stress, suffering with jobs that are demanding and overwhelming. During the strike of air traffic controllers, *Time* ran an essay titled "The Burnout of

Just About Everybody," which questioned whether it was really true that modern life presents us with so many new stresses and pressures that we are crushed under the weight of them. Is it more accurate to say that modern people are less accustomed, and less prepared for, hard, demanding work? I really doubt that the parish ministry is the hardest, most stressful vocation. Many studies indicate that, when stress is measured, parish ministers are in minimally stressful situations. An average day in the average parish is usually not nearly so stressful as a front row seat at a good college basketball game. Stress alone cannot be the key to our burnout problems.

My mother worked for twelve months a year as a teacher. For nine months, she taught home economics from 8:00 A.M. until 4:00 P.M. Then, in the summer, she supervised a school cannery for home gardeners. This involved managing an assembly line operation run by amateurs in steamy heat that regularly rose to over 130 degrees. How did she stand it? I have often wondered. I think she survived, even enjoyed, such work because she had a strong sense that what she did was valuable and intrinsically worthwhile. She felt a keen sense of responsibility and dignity as a teacher. As far as I know, I have never worked a day in my life as a pastor and a professor that was as demanding and physically grueling as one of my mother's days in that summer cannery. Burnout must be related to a wider range of factors than stressful, demanding work loads.

How did we get a generation of seminarians whose great concern is the securing of "space for me?" How did we get those whose first week in the parish is spent negotiating for days off and designing contracts that carefully restrict their obligations to the parish?

"I have simply got to look after me," said one. "If I don't take care of me and my needs, who will?"

I know the peril of over-work, super-sacrifice among clergy. Nothing in this book (unlike the Bible!) asks people to die for the church. (Though I must say that, in my opinion, a person could give up his or her life for much less than the church!)

Perhaps we are dealing with a problem of "over-learning" in the matters of personal leisure time, exercise, spiritual renewal, and personal space. Having heard the message that we do ourselves, our families, and our churches a great disservice by getting on a treadmill of busy, harried activity, some clergy have the erroneous notion that leisure and time off are infinitely more valuable than productivity, conscientious labor, and service to others.

Fran Liebowitz says that whereas the heroes of the sixties were idealists and activists, the heroes and significant people of the eighties are those who rest well. The great achievement, in our own age, belongs to those who don't achieve, but who recreate, meditate, and rest with style. Is there any wonder that "burnout" has become the great social disease of the eighties? Go ahead and burn out; you deserve it!

Susan Littwin, in *The Postponed Generation*, by interviewing today's young adults found a generation of people who were reared by parents who (usually unintentionally) sheltered their children from the hard facts of life, cushioned their every fall. Their parents convinced them that they were special and entitled to

23

the best of life without work, risk, or sacrifice and led them to believe that happiness was their natural right. Now, as young adults, these twenty- and thirty-year-old "children" refuse to grow up, postpone confrontation with reality, and wait for the world to hand everything to them for nothing, much as their hard working parents handed it to them. If any of them find their way into the church (not likely for many of them due to the church's historic stress on commitment and sacrifice), they will find the going rough. Some of the "postponed generation," some in every generation, live under the naive, magical illusion that somehow we shall achieve happiness, character, joy, and fulfillment simply by wanting it.

"I really want to love people, to be with them, to make a real impact on the world with them, but I just can't find a church where people are really serious about discipleship," said a young pastor. It seems not to have occurred to her that such a church doesn't just happen. If there are such churches, they did not spring up overnight, like magic. This pastor will either learn the facts of life—the necessity for hard work in the pastoral ministry—or she will burn out. Ministry is work.

Our culture emphasizes instant gratification of all desires. We are told, in countless television commercials, that we can have what we want and have it now, with push-button ease. Is there any wonder that people, pastors and laity alike, are seeking a "quick fix" for their spiritual emptiness? Television preachers appeal to many who fall for the notion that it is possible to be a committed Christian with deep, abiding faith, in an instant, in a moment, in the twinkling of the eye.

This is a promise of magic rather than ministry. When many of these people find out what the saints have always known—that Christianity is tough, demanding, and requires a lifetime of trial and error, perseverance, and searching self-examination—they feel betrayed and burnout, looking for some other magic, quick fix to cure their ills.

John Sanford suggests that the phenomenon of dissipation and disengagement, which we commonly call burnout, may arise from a lack of *meaning* rather than from a lack of energy. I agree. Both the laity and the clergy go through crises that cause them to pull away from the church, to drop out passively, or to storm out angrily. This book is an exploration of why they do so and what steps we might take to keep people committed to the life and work of the church. It is based on the assumption that people are committed to the institutions that they find meaningful and that they lose their commitment when they no longer find meaning within a given institution such as the church. In other words, people appear to burn out in the church not necessarily because they are overworked, but because they are overburdened with the trivial and the unimportant.

When our commitment dissipates, we do feel as though we are burning out. The least task—visiting a prospective church member, attending a committee meeting, filling out an annual report—becomes drudgery. In the world of work, burnout occurs when energy is expended without fuel being added. In my opinion, the "fuel" that supplies the energy to minister as clergy or lay ministers is a conviction that what we do has meaning. Energy to stay committed arises out of meaningful attachments. When we no longer find meaning in what we do, even the smallest action drains us. Burnout is the result of a lack of meaning.

Factors That Are Unrelated to the Nature of the Church

Let us be clear about some sources of burnout that are not the concern of this book. Many times, clergy and laity fall away from the church for reasons that have nothing to do with the church or with the Christian faith but are simply part of life itself.

For instance, sometimes life crises intrude upon people, rearranging their priorities and loyalties. These crises happen to everyone from time to time. When they do, sometimes we fall away. The death of someone we love, a divorce, a traffic ticket on the way to church, difficulties with our children, unhappiness in our job—all these can consume us and render us ineffective in the church.

Observation indicates that there is a sort of rhythm to people's involvement in the church, or in any other institution for that matter. We have different needs at different periods in our lives. Sometimes the church and its ministry appear to meet these needs; sometimes they do not. In churches I have served, I have noticed a tendency of people to be heavily involved in activities when their children were school aged. Some time after their children reached adulthood, many couples seemed to be less engaged in the church. This pattern continued until about the time of their retirement, when they became active again. Gary Harbaugh, in *The Pastor as Person*, cites studies of levels of satisfaction among pastors and notes that the first three to five years of ministry tend to be the hardest, followed by other critical periods during the eighth to tenth year and then again around the twentieth year of ministry. I expect that we clergy tend to ascribe far too much significance to theological factors in a person's commitment to the church—this person is not really dedicated to the work of the kingdom of God—rather than to psychological, sociological, and life crisis factors—this person is enjoying the new freedom of no longer having total responsibility for her children and wishes to take a "leave of absence" from her church.

It is important for pastors, in their relationships with their parishioners, to recognize when a parishioner's apparent burnout and disengagement from the church arise, not from any lack of faith, commitment, or new dissatisfaction with the church, but rather from normal, predictable life crises or stages. I have seen pastors who immediately assume, simply because someone who attended church frequently is now attending less frequently, that person must be angry with the pastor. People may disengage from the church for a variety of reasons, many of which have to do more with specific, personal needs than with any shortcomings of the church and its leaders.

In fact, some pastors have found that it is important to give permission for parishioners to take a "leave of absence," to let them know that it is not a terrible sin to be less active in the church for a time. Frantic, breathless efforts to get someone back to church may do more harm than good. It is better to keep in touch, to let persons know that we love them, even if we don't see them every Sunday, and to let the normal and predictable rhythms of life take their course.

Of course, pastors are not immune to the same life crises that affect their parishioners. Churches would do well to consider formal leaves of absence and sabbaticals for pastors who experience a personal crisis. Too many times, a conscientious pastor will precipitously leave the ministry during a personal crisis rather than ask for a time away to work things out.

There are times in a pastor's life when—because of personal crises, loss of fervor, health problems, or a host of other difficulties—it is best for that person to leave the pastorate and to serve the church in some other form of ministry. All of us are "ministers" by virtue of our baptism. The pastoral ministry is only one particular form of ministry, but it is one in which a person has been chosen by God and the church to care for a congregation.

Skillful care of a congregation requires a complex of personality traits, skills, emotional and physical stamina, and other characteristics. A person who suffers through some severe personal crisis, despite his or her best intentions and sincerity of effort, may be rendered unable to fulfill the tasks of the pastoral ministry. His or her ministry should now be performed in some capacity other than as a parish pastor.

If persons become pastors in their early twenties, they may have up to fifty years in which to be pastors. In an earlier day, few people lived long enough to devote fifty years to any job. Few of us are equipped to do exactly the same job for many decades without some break in the routine or some intentional change of pace. The notion that someone is a priest forever arises from an outmoded view that sees ministry as a matter of imbued special characteristics residing in an especially *holy person* (the priest) rather than as a matter of someone doing especially *holy work* for the church. The holy work continues even when the people doing the work change.

It is important for churches, particularly at the denominational level, to develop structures to help persons leave the pastoral ministry when the need arises. Counseling—vocational, economic, psychological, spiritual—may help, but it is no panacea. A decision to leave the pastoral ministry will rarely be a painless matter. Yet everyday, persons change professions, make difficult moves, and launch out on new careers. Why should pastors be immune from those moves? Too many clergy develop dependent attitudes in which they expect everyone else to make their vocational decisions for them. (We will have more to say about this matter of pastoral passivity later.) While the church must love individuals, it must also love congregations. Often, a form of "cheap grace" is in effect for pastors when laity and fellow pastors overlook gross incompetence, poor work records, and personal immorality in the name of Christian charity. This is a tragic perversion of Christian love. The church is too important, and leadership of the church too essential, to allow churches to disintegrate and die out of misplaced concern or simple cowardice in facing up to the facts about incompetent, unqualified pastors.

29

Sometimes, the most loving thing a church can do for a troubled, ineffective, or immoral pastor is to help that person summon up the courage to leave the pastoral ministry and to seek some other work.

Could it be that, when there is a scandal in which a pastor has engaged in some great breach of personal or professional morality, the act occurs not only because of the pastor's own moral confusion, but also because of the mystique surrounding ordination—the notion that one is supposed to be a "priest forever" and that one only leaves the pastoral ministry when one is forced out? The immoral act becomes the pastor's excuse for having to leave the pastorate when he or she is otherwise unable to make the decision to leave.

Of course, in speaking about the need for some persons to be helped out of the pastoral ministry, we are talking about the most extreme situations. Most pastors are caring, competent, and dedicated men and women. The concern of this book is how to help the people who often suffer from ordinary frustration, depression, and low morale to keep going in their ministries. These pastors must not be allowed to jump to the conclusion that periodic bouts with depression or frustration are signs that their ministry is on the rocks. If pastors feel that if they are really called of God and are truly dedicated they would never have feelings of inadequacy or depression, let them know that their call to the ministry in no way isolates them from such feelings. Such feelings are normal, predictable, and are even signs of the pastors' sincerity to give God and the church the very best leadership they have to offer.

Death, divorce, marital problems, old age, periodic

depression, and health problems are crises that strike everyone from time to time. Nothing about our membership in the church protects us from the same crises and life changes that affect everyone else. Generally, these are not the concern of this book. Our primary concern is with those factors that are specifically related to life in the church and that may lead to burnout and dissipation of spirit among clergy and laity. Let us now turn to an examination of some of those factors.

Factors That Are Related to Life in the Church

John Sanford and many others have noted some of the unique aspects of life in the church that relate to clergy burnout. While many of these are the special problem of the church's clergy, several apply to the laity, particularly lay leaders, as well. Some factors that are most important, as well as unique, to life in the church follow.

1. *The work of the church is never done.* I enjoy such chores as mowing the grass and painting the house because, as a pastor, I so rarely have the satisfaction of seeing a job through to completion. Most of the things we do are open ended. How do we know if last month's Bible study series really changed anyone's mind? Have we really done all we could do to prevent alcoholism? A surgeon may have a demanding job, but no surgeon is always in surgery. Pastors have no "Miller time," as the commercial puts it, no time when we can step back and say, "We really did a great job on that bridge, didn't we?"

I interviewed a man who works with elementary school teachers. "A good teacher must be content to be a sower rather than a reaper," he said. "Teachers must not expect to see immediate, specific, concrete results of their efforts. If they have any effect on their students, it will show up later in life, long after their students have left them." I think that much the same can be said of the pastoral ministry. The work involves sowing more than reaping.

2. Too much of the time, *the church doesn't give us a clear picture of the expectations and the tasks we are supposed to fulfill.* I remember a dear person who came to me, saying that she wished "to resign from my church office because I feel like a miserable failure." Why did she feel like a failure? She had served for two years as ecumenical affairs chairperson, an office that was mandated by our national church structure. To her knowledge, she had done nothing to fulfill her responsibilities. As we talked, I realized that she hadn't the slightest notion of what those responsibilities were. She was a "failure" before she began.

Most pastors work with ill-defined congregational expectations. They, therefore, feel as though they are always in a "no-win" situation. Expectations for their performance are so diverse and amorphous, related to each individual parishioner's vague picture of what a "good pastor" looks like, that the poor pastor never feels that he or she is doing the job. What is the job?

"I feel like I have six hundred different bosses," said one pastor, "each one holding a detailed job description for me that no one has the decency to show me!"

The laziest persons I know, as well as the hardest

working people I know, tend to be either clergy or professors. The reason is that both the pastoral ministry and academic work are open-ended. The job is never finished. What is the job? There is always someone else to be visited, another book to be read.

As a pastor, time and again I would end my day by closing the church office and saying to myself, "I think I really accomplished a great deal today." Then, when I was on my way home, I would pass by someone's house and say to myself, "I really should have visited that person this week. I haven't seen her since her husband died." Then I would think, "I meant to read that new commentary on Matthew before I started on this week's sermon. Here it is Wednesday, and I haven't even begun." By the time I reached home, I was already depressed and defeated, robbed of any sense of completion and accomplishment.

Reinhold Niebuhr, in his *Leaves from the Notebook of a Tamed Cynic*, describes the parish ministry as

a task which requires the knowledge of a social scientist and the insight and imagination of a poet, the executive talents of a business man and the mental discipline of a philosopher. . . . It is not easy to be all things to all men. Perhaps that is why people are so critical of us. Our task is not specific enough to make a high degree of skill possible or to result in tangible and easily measured results. People can find fault with us easily enough and we have no statistics to overawe them and to negate their criticism. (New York: Meridian Books, 1957, pp. 201-2)

We have defined ministry even less clearly today than when Niebuhr wrote these words in 1928. A particularly problematic situation erupts with the fresh-out-of-seminary associate pastor (especially if he or she is the *first* associate the congregation has had). The senior minister enjoys a relatively well defined, often carefully negotiated role. The associate is expected to do everything else to make up for all the areas of the senior pastor's inadequacy or to be the senior pastor's resident scapegoat.

Because of the ill defined nature of the pastoral ministry, the work demands a high level of internal control. Pastors probably have less peer supervision than any other profession. They are on their own. In conscientious persons, this encourages a heightened sense of responsibility, but it can lead to an oppressive situation if the person is not only conscientious but also perfectionistic and unrealistic.

3. *Ministry tends to be repetitive.* One of the attractions of the pastoral ministry for me was its variety. Pastors enjoy a wide variety of responsibilities and challenges—but only up to a point. A great deal of the pastoral ministry repeats itself. No sooner has one left the pulpit at the end of the sermon than one must begin the next week's sermon. Even as the church's liturgical year keeps reiterating the same days and seasons, like clockwork, year after year, so also there are always lists of sick people in the hospital, prospective members to be visited, and spring confirmation classes. This repetition can be grinding.

4. Related to the above, *ministers must work with the same people year after year.* At my last parish, I realized that I dreaded the annual fall meeting of the nominations committee. I did not mind the first meeting of the

committee, but by my fourth year at the church, I found it very depressing—the same list of the same people for the same jobs. By my fourth year, I already knew all the people who would probably offer lame excuses for why they could not work for the church. I already knew all the ones who would say yes, but then not fulfill their responsibilities.

The laity feel the same way. I have found that one primary justification for church growth is that members become bored with the same people. A church that does not grow does not take in new life. We have already heard all of John Jones' opinions on every issue. We already know how Jane Doe will respond to any suggestion to renovate the fellowship hall.

The first year or two in a new church is exciting and interesting. But after a few years there, we realize that this congregation, for all its strengths, has many of the same weaknesses and problems as any other congregation. This can be depressing.

In addition to this, the same people are also *volunteers*. They choose to be at church, and they can freely choose not to be there. The people with whom we must work in the church are not necessarily the ones we would have chosen if *we* had been hiring laborers for the vineyard!

"I'm quitting!" he shouted at me. "I'm fed up with people who don't come to meetings, don't do what they agree to do, don't follow through with projects." He was an executive with a local manufacturer, a man accustomed to having his way and getting people to do what they were told. Therefore he was miserable as a leader in the church.

5. Because *the church is a haven and refuge for people in great need*, it can be a place of great difficulty for those who attempt to minister to those needs. As is often said, the church is a hospital for those who are sick. Sick, hurting people are often difficult and demanding. They come to the church empty, confused, needy, and hopeful. Many times when we are hurting, we are hostile; we even lash out at those who try to help us, sometimes refusing their help, even while we say we want help. If the church does its job, it probably has a higher percentage of hurting, needy people than does any other institution.

Clergy and laity sometimes wonder why there is so much unpleasantness at church meetings, why people can't seem to get along, why everything—even seemingly small things—can become great, emotionally charged major issues. People in pain are not pleasant to be around.

I remember being trained as a scout lifeguard. "Don't ever jump in the water to save a drowning person," I was advised. "Reach to the person. Throw something. Only dive in as the very last resort when all else fails." Drowning people tend to drown their rescuers, not because drowning people are evil but because there is a natural human reaction for self-preservation. In the church, one meets many drowning people. If you risk getting close to these people, really trying to help them, there is a chance you may go under.

Perhaps this accounts for the superficiality of many congregations. There seems to be an unspoken fear that, if we really talked about our hurts openly and honestly, if we really confronted our problems, they would destroy us. Keep things polite, superficial, and bland. I have no doubt that some pastors substitute superficial back-slapping and jovial conviviality for true pastoral care out of their own subconscious fears that they dare not enter other people's pain lest that pain consume them.

"Why do you want to go into the pastoral ministry?" I ask my students in seminary.

"Because I like working with people," some of them answer.

"Have you met the people?" I ask.

6. *Some people join the church not out of any deep commitment to the true purpose of the church, but rather out of a desire to receive attention and affirmation from the church.* My last parish had a fairly aggressive evangelism program. An older pastor said to me, "Your counseling load will double. Most of these new people will affiliate with your church, and then only for a short time, for all the wrong reasons." Many of them have not joined a church, they have come to an organization that will wave a magic wand over their marriage, make their children behave, and give them great entertainment on Sunday morning.

One couple said to me, "When we were looking for a church, you were at our house nearly every evening. Now that we've joined, we hardly ever see you." I realized that, in my earnest efforts to recruit them for our church, I had misled them into the wrong assumptions about the church. Our "evangelism" had backfired. We had recruited new members, telling them all the wonderful things the church would do for them, without telling them all of the things the church would demand of them. "Come to our church and get a

37

new best friend in Pastor Bob." "Come to our church, where you will meet beautiful people who have perfect marriages and obedient and chaste teenagers, and where the sermons are always stimulating." A sick relationship develops between people who expect their minister to be a "star" or a saint and a pastor who tries to fulfill their unrealistic (and even unchristian) expectations.

When these people join the church and find that the church demands commitment of its members, insists on their giving rather than receiving, and desires them to serve rather than to be served, they become disillusioned and angry. They feel betrayed because they are not receiving the attention and support they expected. The saintly pastor turns out to be just another fallible human being, and they hate the pastor for that humanity.

7. John Sanford notes that persons in ministry, and I assume this also applies to laity in ministry, must function a great deal of the time in what the psychotherapist Jung called the *persona*. The persona is the mask that was worn in ancient Greek tragedy. For Jung, the persona is that psychological mask we put over our real inner feelings when we must relate to others. In the church, we appear to be deeply concerned about people's problem, even when we really aren't. A pastor has a miserable day, comes home to relax, and at about 11:00 P.M. the telephone rings—someone's mother has just died. Even though not feeling like it, the pastor must get up, get dressed, put on persona, and go be a minister.

The persona is not necessarily an act or a deceitful

charade. It helps to protect us by keeping parts of ourselves hidden. It is the "professional" front we must necessarily adopt to fulfill our responsibilities. The pastor isn't being deceitful when expressing sympathy and care for the grieving person, but the pastor puts his or her personal feelings aside in order to accomplish the greater good of offering care to a grieving person.

Yet, the persona can be maladaptive. Too many pastors deny themselves an opportunity to "de-role." They are always pastors. There is no point in the day when they put up their feet and hang up the mask. They go through their entire lives feeling as though they are delicately balancing themselves on a pedestal, desperately attempting to fulfill an impossible ideal. This leads to a life of posturing, suppression of true feelings, and loss of touch with their real selves. Jung felt that the brighter the persona, the darker the shadow underneath. The shadow is that dark, hidden, inner self that the persona shields. This, perhaps, accounts for the many pastors and laypersons in the church who appear to be artificial and fake. It takes a great deal of energy to keep the persona polished and clean. When too much energy is expended in keeping up this mask, when there is no chance to move out of the role and take off the mask and let down the image, psychic damage can result.

Be well assured that this malady affects lay leaders in the church as well as the pastor. Once I tried to talk a man into serving in an important position in our congregation. He steadfastly refused my overtures, offering a series of rather unconvincing excuses for his refusal. When I persisted, he broke down into tears and said, "I can't do this because I am sick and tired of living a lie. I'm not the man that all the people at the church think I am." He then confessed his involvement in an extra-marital affair. If church is never a place for us to confess and to experience our real selves, it can be a miserable place.

8. *Church people may be exhausted by failure.* Earlier, we noted that the church has a way of setting unrealistic expectations for itself. It is no wonder that, at the end of the year, the congregation looks back and often feels defeated, frustrated, and discouraged. Jesus preached away more people than he won. His own disciples disappointed him and eventually forsook him and fled when the going got rough. That same dynamic of disappointment and frustration with the high demands of discipleship and the realities of the human predicament is at the heart of church life. Pastors and laity alike often feel suspended across that great gap between what the church is and what it is called by God to be. This gap—experienced at unpleasant board meetings, in encounters with half-committed members, and in moments when the hypocrisy and downright deceit of persons are felt—threatens our sense of commitment. It is no wonder that we meet many pastors who are cynics, full of cute, cutting remarks about the duplicity of the laity and the clergy. The Body of Christ sometimes seems so invisible!

Richard Baxter, busily prodding seventeenth-century English pastors to work harder and be more faithful, confessed to his own sense of failure to reach his people in his preaching. "I am daily forced to wonder how lamentably ignorant many of our people are who have

40

seemed diligent hearers of me these ten or twelve years while I spoke as plainly as I was able to speak . . . many of our people will be obstinately unwilling to be taught" (See *The Reformed Pastor*, pp. 113-14).

I once asked a distinguished neurosurgeon, half in jest, "Why are all the brain surgeons I know such strange people?"

"What do you expect?" she replied. "About 90 percent of the work we do is either just standing by and watching nature take its course or else a total failure. There is really very little we can do for serious diseases and injuries to the brain. Some days I do nothing but stand by helplessly and watch people die. That does something to a person."

In the church, we also do a great deal of standing by helplessly as people die, as their marriages fail, as their cancer does not heal, as their enthusiasm lags, as their old, self-destructive habits reappear. It does something to us.

"You're a pastor?" a man asked me at a party. "Well, I'm not exactly sure of what you do, but I know that you do people a lot of good." Do I?

9. *The church and its ministry are not valued by the surrounding culture.* The church in America is gradually realizing that it is not the culturally significant institution that it once thought it was. Many of us, particularly those of us in mainline Protestant denominations, conceive of ourselves as the custodians of the nation's civil religion. We were the culturally dominant form of religious expression for most of this nation's life. Who would argue that this is true today?

We live in a culture that values money and that

measures the worth of people by their salaries. The brain surgeon has a demanding, tension-filled, and difficult job, and the surgeon is paid quite well to do it. People may admire what pastors do, but when pastors look at their paychecks, they realize where they stack up on the materialistic totem pole. Even the most altruistic pastors find it difficult not to feel that they are valued less because they are paid less.

In the past few decades, many liberal churches have gone through a frantic attempt to find some socially acceptable function for themselves. They have built gyms, opened counseling services, become centers of political agitation, and so on. Some of this is directly related to the mission of the church. But much of it is also an attempt to regain a place as an approved, appreciated institution in American culture.

The local newspaper runs a story of the church's clothes closet for the poor. The congregation is elated over the recognition by a secular newspaper reporter. One could hardly expect the newspaper to appreciate or even to understand weekly gatherings for worship, and the importance of preaching, fellowship, or prayer and Bible study groups. But the newspaper does appreciate what the church does for its community. "See," the parishioners say, "*we really are* doing something worthwhile here."

Attempts to win the approval of the surrounding, largely secular, culture can be a trap for the church. The theological purpose of the church may be placed in jeopardy in the breathless attempt to be all things to all people, to receive the praise of those who do not hold the church's vision of truth and reality, rather than to adhere steadfastly to the true purpose as defined in scripture and church tradition.

10. Many of us must serve in situations where there is *institutional decline.* My own denomination has lost two million members in less than two decades. That statistic is depressing enough, but when one moves from the denominational to the local church level, the depression is even greater. What does it do to a church to see itself in constant decline? The empty pews, vacant church school rooms, monetary troubles, and leaking roof all take their toll on pastoral and lay morale. Institutional blight leads to despair. Unless things change, the majority of pastors in my denomination will spend most of their ministry time in declining churches.

All of us enjoy being part of a "winning" organization. Every time a family leaves a congregation to join a more active vital one, grief and feelings of rejection and failure afflict the congregation that must bid them farewell. Clerical and lay leadership are apt to burn out or to detach themselves from declining churches to protect themselves from the ravages of slow, gnawing grief and to defend themselves from the feeling that nothing can be done, that commitment to a dying church is pointless.

11. *Much of the church and its ministry is a "head trip."* The church deals with spiritual and intellectual matters, not with fleshly, carnal matters. We come to church to think or to feel, not to be physically active. Most pastors I know are notorious neglecters of their bodies. We may believe in and preach an incarnational faith, but when it

comes to the care and nurture of our own bodies, we live an utterly disembodied docetism.

A national study of Catholic priests indicated that some 70 percent of those studied reported poor skills in interpersonal relationships. Their training had been highly cognitive in nature, even though their priestly work required a great variety of practical skills. Their seminaries had prepared them for a "head trip," but their actual work required a "body/soul/heart trip." (See Gerard Egan, *The Skilled Helper: A Model for Systematic Helping and Interpersonal Relating* [Monterey, Calif.: Brooks/Cole Publishing Co., 1975], pp. 17-18.)

This denial of our own creatureliness easily leads to spiritual and emotional problems. A pastoral counselor says that, when a couple comes to him for counseling, he often tells them, "Next weekend, get a sitter for the kids. Get a room at a good motel. Sit by the pool all day. Sleep late in the morning. Go out for a good dinner in the evening. Dance after dinner. Then, if you still have marital problems on Monday morning, give me a call."

Many times, emotional or relational problems have their roots in neglect of the physical body. A host of studies show that physical activity can greatly reduce levels of stress. Generally speaking, the more cerebral the work, the more we need to nurture our bodies. We are not all brains, not disembodied souls. We are people, creatures, animals who are psychosomatic in all we do. We forget our physicality to our own peril.

12. *Poor time management wears down many in the church.* Church is not the place for the impersonal efficiency of the assembly line. Pastors and laity must be people who take time to care for many people whom

44

the world might consider unworthy of notice. For the Christian, an hour spent visiting a lonely octogenarian may be a more important use of time than an hour spent at a church board meeting. Because of this, it is also true that church people, particularly pastors, are poor managers of time. Many pastors are sinking in a tangled web of trivial, unimportant, poorly organized commitments and activities that rob them of the time they need for more important ministry. Pastors constantly complain that they don't have enough time. Many laity find this complaint incomprehensible. What *does* the pastor do?

I agree with Gary Harbaugh, in his book *The Pastor As Person*, that

> The major frustrations in ministry may be related to two fundamental facts of life: time and space. Stress is produced when a person feels there is never enough time . . . when there appears to be either a too restrictive environment in which to function freely, or a too open-ended environment to manage effectively.

If the pastor did what time management experts recommend and made a log of all activities he or she does in the week, along with the time spent doing those activities, the pastor might be surprised at how time is spent: two hours a day opening mail; an hour a day spent hunting for letters and notes on a cluttered desk; an hour spent going back to the hospital because of failing to check the patient registry during a visit earlier in the morning.

Pastors often complain that laity do not respect their time. Even though the pastor keeps office hours, parishioners wait until the evening to call the pastor at home. Sometimes parishioners make appointments with the pastor and then are an hour late. I feel strongly that pastors must respect their own time before they can expect the laity to respect their time. No layperson can possibly know all that a pastor must do within a given week. The laity cannot be blamed if they do not know how stressful a counseling situation has been earlier in the day. The pastor must take charge of his or her own schedule and let laypersons know what can and cannot be done.

I meet pastors who have a great deal of anger because the laity make, in the pastors' minds, unfair demands upon the pastors' time. Who is to blame for this? The pastor must take charge. Yet, here is the root problem: Pastors are reluctant to make choices, to say no, to manage their own ministries. They complain about stress brought on by a lack of control over their own time, a feeling of impotency and helplessness. At the same time, the laity complain that their pastor wastes time, seems to have no clear objectives or goals, is consumed by trivial tasks and neglects important responsibilities.

Of course, some things are beyond a pastor's control. A pastor may devise a well managed schedule, but must also be willing to junk the schedule when there is an acute crisis in the parish. A pastor cannot plan when people will be seriously ill or in grief, but most pastors can exercise a great deal more control over their own time.

Too many clergy are passive/aggressive in their use of time. They passively agree to all sorts of unrealistic demands upon them, going out to counsel at all hours of the night, neglecting their families, running at the beck and call of their parishioners in the name of pastoral care or deep dedication to ministry. Then they swallow their anger at their feelings of impotency in the face of congregational demands. Their aggression surfaces in a sermon or at the board meeting in ways that are destructive, unprofessional, and have little to do with the real problem, which is the pastor's own inability to say no.

Pastors who refuse to set priorities for their ministry will be at the mercy and disposal of the first persons who call to claim their time. This is not ministry. Sermons will not be prepared; time for study will dissipate; the sick will not be visited; and the pastor's own personal and family commitments will suffer.

Laity can also be victims of poor time management, although I must confess that this seems to be a greater problem for pastors. Church meetings that have no agenda and no leadership or direction are the bane of the laity's existence. Otherwise well organized and efficient people sometimes seem to shed their efficiency and wander into a sort of dreamlike state when they enter the church building. In the name of kindness, meetings are allowed to drag on and on; certain people are permitted to filibuster during discussions; and nothing ever happens. A few evenings of this, and the laity begin to exhibit the same passive/aggressive tendencies as their pastors. A meeting is held, and no one is there. Excuses are made for absences, but the real reason is that the laity have discovered that church—a haven from accountability, direction, and vision—is a waste of time.

13. *Ministry is often a mess.* A pastoral counselor who had spent fifteen years listening to the problems of pastors and their spouses told me that the essential personality requisite for happiness in the pastoral ministry is "a high tolerance for ambiguity. Personalities that put a premium on neatness, exactitude, and order are miserable in ministry. Life is messy; people are mysterious; and few people, once one really gets to know them, fit our labels. No one who has been in business as a printer or a photographer should become a pastor!"

Of course, he said this partly in jest. But his prohibition is fascinating. Printers who must be exact, whose goal is neatness and legibility, will find that parish life is messy. If your idea of life is limited to what you can see through a small hole, with all the action focused and frozen, a church can drive you crazy.

In seminary, I deeply imbibed a theology of grace. God loves us, just as we are. Paul Tillich's sermon on accepting our acceptance was my theme song. But a few months into my first pastorate, I came to the reluctant conclusion that I didn't really believe in acceptance. People, when I got to know them in depth, were a mess. Beneath the neat facades of their Sunday best, demons roamed. I found myself unconsciously wandering about like Abraham, desperately searching for two or three really good people in my messy Sodom. I had to admit that it really did bother me that so few of the people were good, righteous, just, nonsexist, and nonracist. The ambiguity of it all almost got to me.

Of course, it is because of this ambiguity, this mess, this *sin*, that Jesus came. A confrontation with the messiness of life is an excellent occasion to witness to the grace of God. Without grace, we are doomed to cynicism, futile attempts to "clean up" people and the church, or mushy affirmations that down deep, these people mean well and are basically good—all evidence to the contrary.

In my experience, laypeople are often better at living with the ambiguities of people and parish life than are their pastors. Clergy are frequently idealists who expect that, given superior preaching, skillful administration, and wise counseling, people will get their lives together. Many laity are blessed with the mundane realism that urges us to love and to accept people—pains in the neck though they are. What the pastor may regard as premature capitulation to the power of sin, the laity may experience as down-home, everyday living out of grace.

14. The *pastoral ministry requires the commitment, or at least the sympathetic support, of the pastor's spouse.* For most churches, the day when the pastor's spouse was considered to be an unpaid church staff member is over. But congregations still expect, and most pastors still need, a spouse who is supportive of the peculiar demands of the parish ministry. I suppose that a certified public accountant can be married to a spouse who could care less about his or her career, who does not share the values of good accounting practices. But a parish pastor must have the sort of marriage in which the spouse understands and supports the work.

Lack of a spouse's support may be a particular problem even for clergy couples. Picture the young, pregnant pastor, with a two-year-old and a four-year-old, who is married to a pastor who concentrates exclusively on the needs of his own church and schedules little time to be helpful to his wife or to share in child-rearing responsibilities. She is having to "mother" a church, two children, and (sometimes) a husband. Someone will be badly hurt or neglected in the process, and that is often the pastor who is exhausted by her inability to shoulder so much responsibility in so many different areas.

15. *Pastors and laity must be in general harmony with the denominational value system, theological stance, and priorities.* Of course, we may disagree with our church's hierarchy, adjudication, or polity on certain matters. It is fair to fight within the family, but when one no longer feels that he or she is a part of the family, that is a different matter. Pastors and laity must feel that, while they may quibble with this or that denominational program or leader, they are still part of the denomination and are in sympathy with the denomination's general direction. Change in the denomination's direction or personality and change in the personality of the pastor or layperson can lead to a serious break between the individual and the institution.

All of these factors suggest that burnout, brownout, dissipation of energy and commitment—whatever you choose to call what often happens to people in the church—is more a matter of distress than of stress, a lack of meaning rather than a lack of energy. The church shares many of the same human tensions and demands as any other human institution. Yet, because of the peculiar nature of the church and its work, the church also presents its members with some peculiar dilemmas.

It has been the purpose of this chapter to enumerate some of those factors that may lead to church burnout. Now, having explored some of the symptoms and causes of this malady, let us move beyond diagnosis and examine some possible cures.

II

TAKING CHARGE

Preachers are often accused by the laity of preaching sermons that are long on diagnosis of the illness and short on the prescription of a cure. In our listing of causes of burnout among clergy and laity, we mentioned some specific solutions—a leave of absence from church responsibilities, careful attention to time management, and others. Some of the solutions were implied; a pastor who sets aside no time for physical activity is violating much that we already know about good physical and mental health.

In this section, we will look for more specific insights and practical ways to minister to the problem of burnout and dissipation of energy in ministry. This section is based on the premise that dissipation and burnout are predictable and normal reactions to the demands of Christian commitment and involvement and that they can be helped through informed and skillful pastoral care.

Pastoral Leadership in the
Spiritual Care of the Congregation

When I was in seminary, I heard a good deal of criticism of the image of the shepherd and sheep for pastor and congregation. The sheep-shepherd image was said to promote authoritarian, dominant pastors and submissive, passive laity. We students were urged to be quiet encouragers and enablers, standing in the wings, helping the laity to assume their own God-given freedom and autonomy. Under this new image, if some laity fell by the wayside, we attributed their falling away to their own inability to accept their freedom. We couldn't help them unless they really wanted to be helped. We left them to fend for themselves so far as their spiritual needs were concerned, to help themselves to the smorgasbord of pastoral acts we offered. Some found their way to more authoritarian churches, which gladly offered to tell them what to do, to be, and to say. Others simply drifted away, having come to the conclusion that, if anything was to be done about their emptiness, it was up to them as isolated individuals to do it.

I now agree with Alfred C. Krass, who charges that this "laid-back," "take-us-or-leave-us" style of pastoral care owes more to the liberal world view, with its notion of the private, autonomous individual, than it does to a specifically Christian theological perspective. In his article "Growing Together in Spirituality: Pastor and Parish Have a Check-Up," printed in *The Christian Century* (April 1, 1987, pp. 311-14), Krass tells how he led his parish on a spiritual check-up using a questionnaire based on Colossians 1:9-14. As Krass notes, many of us mainline, liberal pastors have uncritically accepted the modern era's relegation of religion to the sphere of the personal and the private, thus capitulating to the radical individualism of the modern world view. My spiritual vitality is my own business. It, therefore, goes against our liberal bias to have firm expectations of what people will do concerning their religious commitments. That is their own private affair, we say. The preacher is here to offer inductive suggestions, images, and his or her own personal insights rather than firm, specific spiritual direction.

This is all the more odd when compared to the fact that most of us mainline, liberal preachers feel absolutely no such reservations about telling people exactly how they ought to respond to certain select social and political issues. We quite readily tell them how to vote on some issues, what position to hold on Central America or nuclear disarmament. But when it comes to prayer, study of scripture, service to others, and examination of personal habits, we say that those are personal, individual matters between them and God. I, like Krass, have come to see this as a capitulation to the spirit of our times. We expect our physician to take authority, to ask questions, to make prescriptions of diet, exercise, or medication when we have a physical check-up. Should we not expect the same sort of directed care from our pastors?

I am convinced that one of the great appeals of the more conservative churches is that many of them offer their people a structure and direction for the spiritual life. As a United Methodist, I am an heir to John Wesley, who had a keen sense that some things—indeed, the most important things—should not be left to chance or to individual feelings, urges, or emotions. The spiritual life could thrive under certain disciplines, methods (hence the name "Methodists"). Pastor Krass used a questionnaire to ask people such things as, "Do you believe that you bear fruit for the Lord, that you live a life worthy of Christ?" He made appointments with his parishioners, gave them the questionnaire, then told them that the responses were for them only to see. After completion of the questionnaire, he led them in a directed pastoral conversation about their own assessment of their spiritual well being, including possible ways to improve it.

Of course, some of his parishioners either refused to make an appointment or repeatedly failed to keep their appointments. But overall, it was a positive experience for the congregation and a signal that their pastor took active responsibility for helping them to grow spiritually. Krass found that "Some people blamed their lack of growth on their relationship to the church. Either they had changed or the church had, and they no longer found it to be meeting their needs. . . . We explored the question of whether that feeling was likely to change or whether, in order to regain their devotion, they ought to look for another church."

To some, he suggested they keep a journal, to others, he recommended a special counselor. One parishioner, who confessed that she had been alienated from another person in the congregation after an argument, was encouraged to take specific steps to reconcile with that person. She did, and reconciliation was effected. What appeals to me in this account of Krass' experiment with the spiritual check up, is the initiative he took as a pastor in offering care to his people. Some pastors act like secular mental health counselors, setting up office hours and sitting back and waiting for their people to come to them for help. A few do come to them, especially those with the most severe personal crises. How do we care for people who go through the day to day crises of fatigue, disillusionment, frustration, anger, and misunderstanding in the church? Krass says, "The check-ups helped me realize how little I knew about the interior lives of many of my parishioners." Pastors who do not take specific steps to listen systematically to their parishioners do not know them.

In a former parish, I led a men's Thursday morning prayer breakfast. Generally speaking, prayer and Bible study at 7:00 A.M. is not my favorite pastime! But I was continually impressed by how this contact with a small group of my parishioners helped me to know them intimately in ways that would have been impossible without the small group contact.

One morning I had been talking about the need to serve Christ in our daily work. Without warning, a young man burst into tears and told the group about the difficulties he had been experiencing at work with his new manager.

"How can I serve Christ with a man like my manager breathing down my neck all the time?" he asked.

The group then had an opportunity to offer support

and encouragement to this brother who was in despair. I was particularly impressed by the way some of the older and more experienced men in the group were able to help.

At another breakfast, a public school teacher discussed his frustrations with his students. After the breakfast, I asked him if he might be interested in forming a support group for public school teachers at our church. Eventually, a group was formed for teachers, a group that enabled me to meet with them for over a year, to learn from them, and to offer them pastoral care in their daily work.

The congregation ought to be a sign to all Christians that they do not have to bear their burdens in isolation. It also ought to be a reminder to the pastor that he or she doesn't have to bear the congregation's burdens alone! If pastors would spend less time in caring for individual parishioners and more time in developing the ministry of individuals within the congregation to others and in forming support groups, the level of care would be greatly increased in the average congregation.

We formed a church school teacher's group that met every month to discuss upcoming lessons, creative teaching methods, and other concerns of teachers. Yet it seemed that we were forever "getting off track" by discussions of frustrations the teachers were experiencing in their classes, such as poor attendance and half-hearted participation. We discovered that these discussions were not pointless diversions, but were the real, if unstated, purpose of our meetings. The teachers needed more support with those frustrations than they did with how to develop lesson plans. So we began

57

intentional efforts to improve our teacher support through the monthly meetings. We developed case studies for group discussion of various problem situations. Outside experts on classroom discipline talked with us. We offered also teacher training, personal Bible study, and other ways to keep teachers teaching.

Pastoral Initiative in Ministry to Burnout

While we have seen that burnout and dissipation of the Spirit is a problem shared by clergy and laity alike, the pastor's own leadership and initiative are crucial in the care of this problem. First, the pastor must display personal and time management habits that demonstrate to the laity that church commitments must be balanced with personal renewal and spiritual growth. If the pastor never takes time for personal retreat and has no regular schedule for personal Bible study, recreation, and study, the pastor's urgings to the laity will fall on deaf ears. Who teaches the laity that it is a sign of spiritual weakness if pastors can't always be present? Unfortunately, it is too often pastors who teach this by their own superhuman efforts to be all things to all people and to be unlimitedly available and accessible to everyone for everything.

Second, remembering the example of Krass' spiritual check-up questionnaire, we pastors need to let our people know that their spiritual well being is part of our responsibility. In our preaching, pastoral care, administration, and teaching ministry, we must hold people accountable to their vision of themselves as Christians.

58

Usually, we cannot wait on the laity to take the initiative in these matters. They may feel a deep, but usually inarticulate, need for more support and guidance from their church, but they are not usually the ones to come up with creative solutions to the problem of dissipation of Spirit. It takes courage to open the door into our deepest thoughts, to suggest that our relationship with God is not all that it could be, and to assess honestly our Christian commitment.

Perhaps we have so many passive, disengaged pastors and so many trivialized, superficial churches because it is painful to dive below the surface. Who knows what demons will be unleashed? What carefully hidden secrets will we discover about ourselves? The pastor must take the initiative in offering a wide range of means for the recovery of corporate discipleship in our day. Of course, we must respect the pluralism, the individuality of persons, and the wide range of personal needs within the congregation. But we can exercise more authority and initiative in fostering communal support for those who struggle to be faithful to their Christian commitments.

Is part of our problem our devaluation of our distinctive role as pastoral upbuilders of the congregation? We have witnessed a blurring of the distinctive ministry of the laity with the ministry of the clergy. Perhaps this blurring has accelerated the problem of dissipation of Spirit for both groups.

All Christians, by virtue of their baptism, are laity, members of the God's family, the *laos*, or people of God, through baptism. At baptism, all of us are given the gifts and graces we need for ministry in the world in the name of Christ. Yet, at an early date, the church found it necessary to set apart some of these "ministers" for the specific ministry of caring for the congregation, empowering and equipping the whole people of God for God's work in the world. These priests, or pastors, did what was necessary to equip the church—including preaching, teaching, guiding, and sustaining—although it was never intended that even these internal congregational functions would be carried on exclusively by the clergy.

Great harm has been done in our day by a blurring of roles of clergy and laity, so that we have laity acting like clergy and clergy acting like laity. Christians who are selected by God and the church to be clergy have their primary ministry within the congregation. The primary ministry of the laity, the people of God, is in the world. Priests and pastors function primarily within the church so that the laity may be about their ministry in the world.

Whenever priests or pastors engage in some ministry outside of the congregation, they do so as laity. I agree with John Westerhoff when he says that when priests work, say, in a soup kitchen or a community home for the homeless, they should take off their clerical collars. They should make clear that they function there as laity, as baptized Christians, doing the ministry that is expected of all baptized Christians, rather than as specially ordained clergy. Anyone who engages in ministries outside of the parish—in counseling, politics, education, community service—does so as a member of the *laos*.

Many of our clergy are spending too much time doing

work that the laity should be doing, work outside the concerns of upbuilding and equipping the congregation, work that the laity should be doing by virtue of their ministry. Many pastors do such work—running for the school board, teaching a course at the local college, political lobbying—because of the implicit assumption, so prevalent among mainline, liberal clergy, that the American church does not need careful, sustained, long-term nurture because the church lives in a relatively Christian culture. Improving the culture in general becomes more important for them than strengthening the church in particular.

This is a dangerous assumption. Clergy need not succumb to the imperialistic assumption that someone has ordained us to care for the whole town, as if the whole town were Christian. Forming a faithful congregation and sustaining faithful Christians in our American culture is quite enough work for a pastor.

Often "lay ministry" means running errands for the pastor, hanging around at the church at all hours rather than being about ministry in the world. Pastors become the surrogate Christian representatives in the community, exhausting themselves by trying to run here and there doing ministry that the laity ought to be doing. Laity become second-class citizens at the church, amateurs, waiting for something useful to do. It is no wonder that we have an overabundance of clergy in many of our denominations and a clericalism that manifests itself in two ways: depreciation of the laity and their call to minister and the appreciation of the clergy in the ridiculous expectation that they will minister for everyone.

I wonder if this confusion is a theological source of much of our lay and clerical burnout. The clergy are exhausted by trying to do everyone else's ministry. The laity are frustrated by the trivialities of confining their ministry to keeping house at the church. If pastors spend more than a day a week engaging in activities beyond the building up of the parish and its people, neglecting pastoral responsibility and if laypersons spend more than fifteen hours per week at the church, they are probably confused about where their main ministry is.

If the clergy are to be effective in the church, the laity must be engaged in the world as Christians, constantly bringing the frustrations, exhilaration, and demands of worldly ministry with them to church so that their pastors might minister to them. If the laity are to be effective in the world, their pastors must be effective equippers and sustainers for them in the church. The focus of the laity is on sharing Christ's ministry to the world rather than being overly preoccupied with the church. The focus of the clergy is to be concerned with the building up of the church rather than to be distracted by the world.

The Courage to Say No

Perhaps our theological confusion about ministry is behind the frequently noted inability of pastors to say no. Pastoral work need not be so diffuse and ill defined as we make it appear. The inability to say no arises when we are unsure of who we are and of what we are supposed to be doing. We say yes to everything out of the fear that we may say no to the thing we truly ought to be doing.

The ability to say no begins with the inner certainty that our role as equippers and builders of God's people is essential, important, and uniquely ours to fulfill. Of course, we are not alone in our ministry to the congregation. We may at times be coordinators of the building up rather than its sole activators. Nor does this mean that we define the nature of pastoral ministry solely on the basis of our own opinions and commitments. Only through constant listening, negotiation, and self-examination with the laity can a pastor really know what his or her job is within this specific congregation. After all, the needs of the world evoke the specific needs for ministry from the laity, and we cannot minister as pastors to the needs of laity unless we are mutually clear about their needs.

Because our pastoral roles are not clearly defined, pastors must be ever vigilant against the tendency to let the important things crowd out time for the utterly essential things. The larger the parish, the less discretion the pastor has over his or her time and the greater the need for the pastor to set careful priorities in order to avoid being drowned in a sea of whatever-happens-to-hit-us-first-in-the-morning.

At every turn in the road, pastors must ask themselves, "Can anyone else in this congregation do this job better?" Every time pastors take over an area of ministry that someone else in the congregation could be doing, the pastors are robbing the laity of their rightful ministry.

When pastors are uncertain about the intrinsic worth

of their vocation as enablers of the congregation, they trivialize their time. They waste hours in unproductive meetings, letting conversations drag on longer than necessary because they have no overriding self-understanding that helps them to organize their time. They have no goal in mind for their ministry. A sort of "Pharisaism of the calendar" takes hold of us, and we say to ourselves, "I must be doing ministry here, my calendar is full." We follow the letter of the law, busying ourselves in an endless round of activity without fulfilling the spirit of truly pastoral ministry.

"Let me see your appointment book," said one time management consultant. "And I will have an accurate picture of your deepest values."

Once again, what is said of pastors can also be said of the laity. Laity, like pastors, must set their personal limits on the basis of a thoughtful assessment of their unique gifts and graces as well as the particular needs for ministry in this time and place. The person is wise who is able to say from past experience, "I would like to help you out on this one, but I have discovered that it is just not something I do well. I'll help organize the meeting, because that's something I do well, but I will not give the address."

Laity can suffer from the same notion that, because we are called by God and because the work of the church is God's work and because we want to be good servants, we find it impossible to say no. People and pastor burn out and drop out from the inability to say no, an inability that arises from both our lack of theological understanding of our particular ministry

64

and a lack of honesty about our own particular gifts and limitations.

Passivity in the Pastor

If I were to isolate the one factor that seems to predominate in parishes in which there are major problems between the pastor and the people, that factor would be *pastoral passivity*. This theme has cropped up frequently in our exploration of burnout and dissipation of Spirit. Let us look at it now in more detail.

Few of us go into the pastoral ministry out of a love for confrontation, aggressiveness, and assertiveness. When compared with those men and women who enter business, law, or even medicine, we clergy appear to be rather mild mannered and passive. To put it more positively, we are peacemakers, on the side of reconciliation and acceptance rather than confrontation and divisiveness. Generally, these are positive qualities in a pastor, but the church also expects its pastors to be leaders. While Jesus was clear that our leadership in the church is to be different from that of the "Gentiles" who lord over others with displays of power and authority (Mark 10:42), there is no way to lead without the ability to take an active leadership role. The passive pastor, sitting in the wings and waiting for the laity to take charge, to catch a vision, to move, is not usually the empathetic, servant-minded, nonauthoritarian leader he or she pictures himself or herself to be. More often this pastor is someone who has rather arrogantly refused to serve the church by leading the church. After all, if the pastor never pushes any new ideas and never attempts to rally the parish behind some new cause or program and is never critical or impatient with present arrangements, then that pastor will never be blamed when things don't turn out. Passivity is a means of self-protection. (See Lyle Schaller, *Activating the Passive Church* [Nashville: Abingdon Press, 1981], pp. 71-97.)

In a 1985 survey of four hundred pastors in the Minnesota United Methodist Conference, Susan Harrington Devogel found significant strains on their morale ("Clergy Morale: The Ups and Downs." *The Christian Century* [December 17, 1986]: 1149-52). Among the most frequently mentioned sources of low morale were unfair demands made by the church on the pastor's family and spouse, loneliness, reluctance to share openly and deeply with peers, conflict management, volunteer recruitment, and administrative problems in the parish. Devogel noted that, along with these areas of stress, "There is often a tendency, accompanied by a great deal of anger, to blame one's ills on the 'system.' " According to Devogel, organizational researchers have observed that systems that by their very nature foster dependency tend to produce a sense of powerlessness in those who work within them. Clergy are made passive by structures and living arrangements that encourage passivity.

When I began to teach in a seminary, I was quite unhappy with a number of aspects of the administration of the school. One day, I complained to a senior colleague. He told me, "I've found that the more I concern myself with what I'm paid to do here, the happier I am. The more I worry about what the dean and the president are doing or not doing, the more miserable I am. So I've found it helpful to remind myself that I am hired to teach, to do research, and to write. Others are paid to worry about everything else, so I am free to do what I was hired to do. I would suggest that if you are unhappy, you should sit down and list on paper everything that you need to do as a professor here but are denied the opportunity because of something done by the dean or the president. Then go to them and demand that they let you do what you need to do. If they won't let you, quit."

I got the point. When all was said and done, everything I needed to be an effective professor was mine already. I was already free to teach, to write, and to do research. My complaints about the administration of the school were little more than my own cop out for not taking responsibility for my own affairs.

Let us beware of the trap of failing to confront and to fulfill our own responsibilities, of blaming someone else at the top. "If the Bishop were more open to change. . ." "If my Board were only more theologically enlightened. . . ." What do we really need to do in ministry that someone else is keeping us from doing?

A bachelor friend of mine once commented to me that there is only one luxury that married people enjoy that singles are denied. "There is no one there to blame things on," he said. "You can't imagine what a privilege it is for you to be able to say to your wife, 'If only you had let me,' or 'If it hadn't been for you. . . .' "

As is often the case where there is human passivity, the clergy's sense of powerlessness is converted into hostility toward the system or its management.

Devogel comments, "While pastors blamed the 'system' (either the denomination or the local church), there seemed to be a general inability to take responsibility for one's self and one's own happiness." While few clergy (less than 13 percent) indicated that they would consider leaving the pastoral ministry if given the opportunity, one wonders how to empower the rest to improve their own morale and to break through the passivity that so stifles their work. Simply naming the causes of distress and being honest about certain realities of parish ministry, as well as certain limitations in our own personalities, can help. Perhaps because pastors really are protected from some of the demands of business or other professions, they tend to have romantic, unrealistic ideas about life elsewhere. The grass seems greener in someone else's pasture because clergy know little about the unpleasant realities that abound in any job.

We must come to see ourselves as persons with choices rather than as helpless victims. Clergy support groups can be invaluable aids in helping clergy to summon up the strength to take charge of themselves and their lives. Career development counseling can help ministers to develop realistic professional and personal goals and to stop fantasizing about how much better off they would be if the "system" would only stop hindering them. Devogel states:

> Clergy need to be aware that they are not as powerless as they often perceive themselves to be—victims of the ecclesiastical system and the whimsy of the local church. By taking responsibility for their own psychological well-being, social needs, spiritual growth and

professional development, clergy can do a great deal toward creating a more positive professional experience, and a happier personal life for themselves and their families.

On Learning to Do What We Enjoy the Least

When my seminary students present case studies of their most unpleasant situations in their parishes, the confrontations usually center around questions of the power and authority of the pastor. Many of the students confess to being totally unprepared for the exercise of administrative leadership. In the early sixties, Samuel Blizzard studied how Protestant clergy spent their time and how they felt about it. Of the six functional roles within ministry (pastor, teacher, preacher, priest, organizer, and administrator), he found that pastors spent most of their time in the job they liked the least—administration took almost 40 percent of their time. Blizzard found that not only did they not like this work, but also that they did not think they did administrative work well. Thus they felt trapped and inadequate approximately 40 percent of the time!

If parish pastors were studied by Blizzard today, the findings would probably be similar. As we said earlier, burnout in ministry results from a lack of meaning rather than from a lack of energy. A satisfying ministry springs from the conviction that what we are doing is important; it is meaningful to God even if it is foolish to the world.

Every job has certain unpleasant aspects. Sometimes it helps simply to be realistic and admit that, although we pastors do not enjoy administration, it is part of the job. A lifetime spent complaining or wistfully hoping that someday we might find a pastoral position that would leave us free to do nothing but preach and counsel would be a lifetime of frustration. Sometimes we clergy are prone to unreal thinking. We expend too much energy thinking about how things ought to be rather than accepting certain realities. Of course, this envisioning can be an essential trait for good preaching and even good administration. But our visionary side must not overtake our realism.

I remember that when I was first ordained as a United Methodist minister I complained a great deal about our parsonage system. I had never lived in someone else's house, and I thought of a hundred things wrong with the arrangement. Then a wise, if tough-minded, old pastor told me, "Look, if you stay a Methodist preacher, your family will always live in a parsonage. There is no use complaining about it. That's the way it is. It's the system that works best for our church. So that's the way it is."

Although his words were not easy to hear, he was absolutely right. I needed to accept what was possible and to quit worrying about the impossible in order to balance my individual preferences with the institution's necessities. A bishop from the Midwest told me that his pastors recently indicated on a survey that 70 percent of them desired to be appointed to a thriving urban or suburban parish. Yet, in his area only 10 percent of the churches are located in such situations. "This means that about 60 percent of my clergy will spend the majority of their ministry in parishes where

70

they are miserable," the bishop commented sadly. Clergy must learn to accept certain realities or else take steps to move into vocations that present them with other realities.

I have taken somewhat similar advice in regard to my own administration. Administration is still far from my favorite pastoral activity. Knowing this, I try to get my administrative duties over with as quickly and efficiently as possible early in the day. Then I will have the rest of the day free to do what I really like and that I feel I am primarily called to do. In other words, I think that I am a reasonably good administrator because I dislike administration!

Of course, we can become better administrators. Perhaps we might really enjoy the way we spend 40 percent of our time if we were really confident and skilled at this task. A pastor of my acquaintance was appointed to a large congregation, larger than he had ever served before. His first week there, a group of laypeople, business executives, met with him and told him, "We are going to give you a gift you need, whether you think so now or not. We are going to send you away to the management training institute that trains our executives. We are going to see that, unlike most of our previous pastors, you are a good enough manager that you will still have some time to be our pastor."

Many times, administration is so terribly laborious to us because we are not good at organizing our work, making schedules, managing our time, and delegating tasks to others. It helps all of us to know, as accurately as possible, which pastoral jobs we do well and which we do poorly, which jobs we need to do first in the day and which we need to save until such time as they can be enjoyed to their fullest extent. We also need to know which jobs we do so terribly that it is best for us to avoid them altogether through delegating them to someone else. For instance, although I think it is fine for a pastor to be a skillful accountant and financial manager, I am definitely not one. This means that, early on at any new church, I tell the laity that one of them will need to handle that aspect of administration for me, if it is to be done well. Fortunately, there has always been a skilled accountant and monitor of budgets, so here was yet another area of ministry that could be skillfully assumed by the laity—and here was another pastor who managed to be much happier in ministry!

Among the resources that have helped to sharpen my management skills are Lyle E. Schaller's *Effective Church Planning* (Abingdon Press, 1979) and Richard G. Hutcheson's *Wheel Within the Wheel: Confronting the Management Crises of the Pluralistic Church,* (John Knox, 1979).

A Word About Committees

In conversations with laity about the most degrading, grinding aspect of their work in the church, I find that one of the most frequently mentioned problems is their hours of service on poorly organized and seemingly pointless committees. To some extent, this is also a frequently heard complaint of pastors as well. However, some pastors seem positively to enjoy their time spent on church committees, frequently for question-able reasons that have been cited in chapter 1. Hours of committee meetings can give the illusion that something is really happening at a church, that the pastor is really doing his or her job. A pastor who manages to fill up every evening with a committee meeting at the church doesn't have to find anything more important to do. Perhaps this accounts for the frequently heard complaint from the laity that they go to too many meetings in which the pastor is in charge and there is no agenda, no goal, and no real direction to the meeting.

I have heard horror stories from business executives who spend their days making decisions concerning million dollar payrolls and then go to church in the evening to find themselves in a two-hour discussion about whether or not to plant fifty dollars worth of azaleas in front of the church. Of course, there are church leaders who do not have positions of power in business. The lengthy discussion about azaleas is a chance for them to assume responsibility and to exercise power in their church. This is important. Church is an excellent place for the powerless to have some power over their lives. Perhaps this helps to explain why church fights are often so bloody; people who have very little influence over their lives enjoy exercising what little influence they do have in the church to its fullest extent.

I am not so concerned about those people, although the pastor ought to want everyone to do the maximum amount of truly worthwhile and valuable work. I am concerned about some of our most talented members who complain about the trivialization of time and programs through pointless committee work in the church. This trivialization is a major reason for lay dropouts from church leadership.

Norman R. DePuy ("Responsibility and Authority in the Church." *The Christian Ministry* [March 1987]: 7-9) feels that church members who lack administrative skills should, if at all possible, not be asked to serve in the administrative committees of the church. Let them exercise their power elsewhere. A church committee is certainly not the only way to serve the church. Church organization is a means of accomplishing the mission of the church. When it becomes an end in itself, boredom sets in, and the mission of the church becomes a trivial affair of keeping machinery oiled and going to meetings. Even as the pastor can substitute going to meetings for true pastoral ministry, the laity may also attempt to avoid more meaningful service by substituting time on a committee. What can we do to avoid this grinding, degrading, trap?

First, we can simply cut back on committees. Most congregations can function quite well with a bare minimum of organization, particularly our smaller congregations. Too many denominations still prescribe organizational structures for local congregations on the basis of denominational bureaucratic standards rather than on the basis of the needs of a local congregation. Churches that are over-organized have too many committees, which are full of lists of names that have no real, significant function to fulfill in the mission of the congregation. We sandbag people onto these committees simply to fill up the prescribed spots. Need we wonder why these people gradually fall away?

Second, a pastor must set administrative priorities,

74

even as the pastor must set priorities for any area of ministry. Does the pastor need to be at every meeting held in the church? Is the pastor there only out of his own sense of insecurity, his own inability to let go and let the laity make some real decisions for themselves? In my last church, I went to only one meeting of the church Board of Trustees. At that meeting, they spent an hour discussing what to do about the leaking roof. It was a most important hour of discussion, and it was directly related to the mission of the church. However, it was an hour in which I, utterly inexperienced in matters of roofing, had nothing to contribute. From then on, I asked the trustees to keep me informed about their important work by means of typed minutes. This left them free to use their talents, and it freed me to use mine.

Third, nominations committees should be told to put no more people on a committee than there are gifted people to be on that committee. They should also be told to give no more than one significant office to each person in the congregation. If there are not enough people to staff all of the denomination's prescribed committees in the congregation or to do all the things a "successful" congregation is expected to do, forget about those committees. Also, nominations committees should be engaged in systematic, continuing efforts to survey the interests and talents of the congregation. With church computers, a talent bank is relatively easy to compile and to consult when a need for diverse talents arises. Matching the right people to the right jobs is one of the most important ways to keep good people from becoming discouraged.

I am unimpressed with the argument that it is great for persons to be on church committees just to involve those persons, by their mere presence, in the "process" of the congregation's decisions. Vague, ill defined notions of "process" are too often a cover for simple incompetence to administer committees well. Democracy is a great thing, but not all decisions require everyone's opinion. Many decisions are not helped by endless hours of debate and consideration of every possible point of view. Sometimes those who are concerned that every aspect of process is honored are doing little more than disguising their own manipulation of procedures for their own ends. Churches, so concerned to use the gifts of everyone, so sensitive to everyone's feelings and attitudes about every issue, are particularly susceptible to having their work bog down in process as everyone is heard and consulted while nothing gets done. Ultimately, this is degrading and causes disillusionment.

III

FINDING MEANING IN MINISTRY

Earlier, in chapter 1, we noted that ministry generally is not valued by our culture. The local Civic Club may have its "Clergy Appreciation Day," and at times we pastors may feel the respect or admiration of people in the community—depending mostly on how well they know us or how much our ministry touches their lives in particular—but we must admit that pastors, priests, and other church leaders are not seen as the movers and makers of our society. Name one popular television program, Broadway play, or recent movie in which clergy have been depicted in a favorable light. Television programs that would be driven off the air for presenting physicians, minorities, women, or school teachers in an unfavorable light routinely present clergy as either bumbling buffoons or sleazy Elmer Gantrys. Of course, television, cinema, and the theater are rarely accurate depictions of reality, but they do mirror many of our cultural stereotypes and preconceptions, and this society's image of clergy is none too affirming of the clergy themselves.

Few clergy look to the movies or television programs to validate their ministries. Yet we must all look *somewhere* for validation and affirmation of our work. In their best-selling book *In Search of Excellence*, Peters and Waterman repeatedly stress that successful American companies are those that affirm their most creative and talented employees. They tell of ways in which successful companies search for rewards and incentives for their best people. Many times the rewards are not in the form of higher pay. Something as simple as a little lapel pin or a mention of someone's contributions in front of other employees may be all that is needed. To some of us, such affirmation may seem insignificant, but all of us live by the "strokes" we receive. We all respond positively to praise.

The Need for Affirmation

I was impressed, in my conversations with those who counsel clergy, by the fact that a lack of affirmation was the most frequently mentioned reason given for clergy burnout. One veteran counselor told me, "Too many clergy have this almost magical expectation that if they are called by God to be ministers, they don't need the normal, everyday, strokes everyone else needs. They think that their vocation alone is enough to sustain them. Clergy must have more mundane means of support."

It is clear that *the church could do more to affirm its clergy*. I sometimes think that congregations get the clergy they deserve—that is, a complaining, demanding, uncaring congregation is usually rewarded by a defensive, complaining pastor. Likewise, I can testify from experiences in my own ministry that some congregations eventually end up with a better person than the one who was hired as their pastor because of the congregation's love and encouragement.

We lose some of our best clergy because of poor systems of clergy peer support. Young pastors find themselves in remote parishes with absolutely no peer guidance or encouragement. Older pastors feel trapped in situations in which they would like a change but see no way out. At times, as Lyle Schaller has often noted, we reward our failures and punish our successes—that is, we gradually grind down some of our most creative clergy, who then become frustrated or disillusioned in their attempts to move the church forward. Often we are left with clergy who have little incentive, personal vision, or spiritual energy, whose thick skins and low expectations enable them to endure the mediocrity of the church.

The church would be wise to seek out for recognition those clergy who do their jobs well, to recognize them and elevate them as models for other clergy. In some ways, competence is its own reward—but never entirely. Laity sometimes underestimate how much it means to their pastor to hear a word of appreciation or encouragement from them. "Do you know what it does to a person," a pastor once told me, "to work about ten to twelve hours a week on preaching, to give it your very best efforts, and then to go for weeks without one single positive comment or even negative feedback?"

Earlier, we spoke of the need for clergy support groups. Yet support from peers seems to be outside the reach of most clergy. Too many of us work with a "Lone Ranger" sort of mentality, acting as if the need for support and peer encouragement is a sign of weakness or a signal that there is something wrong with our own sense of vocation. Many clergy work in rather isolated situations in which geographical or other factors make it difficult to seek out peer support. Sometimes clergy, though they would be the last to acknowledge it, are in competition with one another for members or for prestige in the community or for denominational advancement. Therefore, they view other clergy as competitors rather than as potential friends. All of these factors can make the pastoral ministry a lonely enterprise, bereft of ongoing support and encouragement, peer review, mutual growth, and a prime target for burnout.

There are a number of reasons—having to do with the nature of the pastoral ministry and with the nature of pastors as persons—why it is unrealistic to expect a spouse, family, friends, and parishioners to provide pastors with their sole means of vocational support and guidance. We need to be with other clergy or perhaps a group of other helping persons such as social workers or physicians and so forth, to whom we may give support and from whom we can receive support.

Related to these observations is a more general one: *clergy must find some means, outside their immediate parish responsibilities, whereby they receive satisfaction, recreation, and support.* As one counselor to clergy put it, "You need to get your kicks from somewhere other than the people to whom you minister." The people of one parish, no matter how good they are, cannot fulfill all of

80

our needs for love, fun, encouragement, and support. In fact, asking them to do so leads to a sort of perversion of our relationship, in which pastor and people become terribly confused and think that the sole purpose of the church is the care and feeding of the pastor. Any leadership role, no matter how humble or dedicated the leader, tends to set the leader apart from those who are led.

Anyone who is a full-time, twenty-four-hours-a-day, seven days a week pastor isn't much of a pastor. The demands of the parish ministry are simply too great for any mere human being to fulfill them without regular opportunities for recreation and renewal outside of the parish; it may be a day a week for fishing or a regular day set apart for retreat and prayer. You may even just spend an hour or so at the end of each day, tinkering with antique automobiles or gardening.

Any worthwhile activity that removes us from the tug and pull of parish responsibilities, even if just for a few hours a week, can be a means of renewal. I am fortunate in my ministry because I am able to make periodic travels to speak or do workshops elsewhere. I receive "strokes" from those who invite me, but the main value is simply in getting away. It does a world of good to be reminded that the whole future of the kingdom of God does not rise or fall on the basis of what happens or doesn't happen at my church. A whole world is out there, full of people who have never even heard of my church. A whole church is out there, where people know nothing of my world. For some reason, this experience of detachment enables me to go back and engage the tasks of ministry at my church with renewed dedication.

Perhaps this is why Carlyle Marney was fond of saying that "Every preacher needs to have something he or she can do when it's time to call it quits on being a pastor." Marney felt that it is important for each of us to have, in the back of our minds or in our suitcase of abilities, something to do should it ever become necessary not to be a pastor. Of course, relatively few pastors will actually leave the parish ministry and do something else. But it is stifling to our spirits to feel that we totally depend on the parish for our future, to feel that calling it quits is never a live option.

Sometimes, quite frankly, we must call it quits. It takes great wisdom to know when to go and when to stay. I worry about the pastors who precipitously leave the ministry altogether when what they may need is a sabbatical or a change of parish. I also worry about congregations who suffer with a pastor who really needs to move on. How many cases of burnout are in reality cases of someone needing to move on? Even one so dedicated and compulsive as Richard Baxter, who thought that nearly all pastoral problems could be cured by harder work and more dedication, admitted in an unguarded moment,

> I confess, for my part, I marvel at some ancient, reverend men that have lived twenty or forty or fifty years with an unprofitable people, among whom they have seen so little fruit of their labors that it was scarce discernible, how they can, with so much patience, there go on. Were it my case, though I durst not leave the vineyard, nor quit my calling, yet I should suspect that

it was God's will I should go somewhere else, and
another come in my place that might be fitter for them.
And I should not be easily satisfied to spend my days in
such a sort. (*The Reformed Pastor*)

Much that we have said about the need for the
affirmation and support of pastors can be applied to the
laity as well. Pastors who are successful at engaging the
laity in ministry are those who apply generous and
regular doses of praise and affirmation. Perhaps
because we are paid to work for the church, it is so easy
for us to take for granted all the other Christians who
serve the church for nothing. We are at the church all
week, so we don't realize how amazing it is for
someone to be there all day on Sunday as a church
school teacher and youth counselor.

It is my practice to write letters to all of my church
officers around Christmas time to thank them for their
work and faithfulness during the year past. I write
these letters in lieu of other Christmas cards. In each
letter, I try to identify some specific reason why I, as
pastor, am grateful for that person's work. At each
church where I have done this, I have been amazed by
how many people tell me that they had never received
thanks, in the form of a note or anything else, for their
work at the church. Do people really know how much
we, as pastors, value and respect how they use their
gifts?

Likewise, the pastor, better than any other Christian,
ought to know how much people need systems of
support and encouragement in their ministry. I
remember a conversation I had one evening with our
choir director and some of the members of our

congregational choir. They expressed a good deal of frustration in their work. "No one in this congregation appreciates how many hours of work we put into five minutes of music on a Sunday morning," one of them said.

"Well, I appreciate it," I said. "I doubt that many in the congregation know the hours I spend preparing for a twenty-minute sermon." In further conversation, we realized how much we, as pastor and musicians, have in common. If laity are often frustrated and feel unappreciated or unaffirmed in their diverse ministries, the pastor should be the leader in ministering to the ministers.

Desperately disillusioned in the wilderness trek, Moses spoke for all of us pastors when he cried to God, "I am not able to carry all this people alone, the burden is too heavy for me" (Num. 11:14). In response, the Lord told Moses to gather seventy elders of Israel, "And I will take some of the spirit which is upon you and put it upon them; and they shall bear the burden of the people with you, that you may not bear it yourself alone" (Num. 11:17).

We need to qualify what we have said about affirmation. None of this means that we should affirm incompetence in either clergy or laity. *Incompetence must be addressed and ministered to rather than ignored.* Certainly, the church is a volunteer organization, and it is to be a place of forgiveness and grace. But it is difficult for the church to be an instrument of God's grace when it tolerates blatant incompetence in its leaders, be they clergy or laity.

Under the guise of graciousness, patience, or

tolerance, we often allow people to remain in positions they are unqualified or uninterested in holding. When we do this, we not only fail to affirm and minister to the people who deserve good Christian education, good preaching, good administration, and wise and prudent management of their financial gifts, but we also miss opportunities to help some fellow Christian struggle with his or her true vocation. Often, the person knows that he or she is in the wrong place, doing the wrong job in the wrong way. By ignoring the problem, we are ignoring the person.

"Nobody likes potential conflict," one pastor told me. "But I feel that a pastor must sometimes say to people, 'You have too much to offer for me to let you get by with this. What's the problem?' Often, I find that we have a good person who, out of a sincere desire to serve the needs of the church, has agreed to be in the wrong position. Or maybe the job was right ten years ago but not now. I always expect that person to resent me for bringing up the problem, but more often than not, he or she is flattered that I think enough of the person and his or her gifts not to ignore them."

Motivation Arises from Meaning

Perhaps a warning should be sounded at this point. The need for affirmation is a basic, human need. Pastors, from what I have observed, tend to have a great desire to please and to be accepted by others. Sometimes, a pastor's description of himself or herself as someone who "likes to work with people" or "enjoys helping people with their problems" may be translated as: "I am a person who needs the praise, gratitude, and support of others." This can lead to a lonely, driven existence as the pastor rushes here and there, desperately trying to please everyone. Somehow, we must develop within ourselves and our ministry an autonomous, inner conviction that what we are doing is worthwhile.

A primary purpose of the church is to provide meaning for its members. People rightly expect their church to help them make sense of life and to provide practical help for getting on in the world. Some time ago, ethicist James Gustafson called the church "a community of moral discourse." That may sound a bit academic, but is it not an accurate description of what it feels like to be in a functioning church?

Perhaps this explains why some of the most effective pastors possess strong intellectual appetites. They may not think of themselves as intellectuals, but they are. They are at home in the world of ideas, are not threatened by the novel and the unconventional, are forever trying to figure out what's going on. Few congregations will admit to desiring an "intellectual pastor." None of them need an armchair academic as pastor. But all of us need help with making sense out of life as Christians. Pastors who enjoy that task, who are always on the prowl for handles, insights, concepts, and models for thinking life through, will never be bored in the parish.

In *The Reformed Pastor*, Richard Baxter, after urging the need for study for his fellow pastors, warns, "Take heed to yourselves lest you perish while you call upon others to heed of perishing, and lest you famish yourselves while you prepare their food."

At the beginning of this exploration into the causes and cures of burnout, dropout, and dissipation of commitment in the church, it was suggested that what appears to be burnout is more a problem of a lack of meaning than a simple lack of energy. Gary Harbaugh claims that "Most of the problems pastors experience in the parish are not caused by the pastor forgetting he or she is a pastor. Most difficulties pastors face in the parish arise when the pastor forgets that he or she is a person" (*The Pastor as Person*). Elsewhere, Harbaugh says that "Studies of the transition from the seminary to the parish—and other studies that have followed pastors through their careers—suggest three major answers to the survival question: self-care, a psychological support system, and self-awareness. The last of these is of first importance" ("Surviving and Thriving in Ministry." *The Christian Ministry* [July 1987]: 24).

I think that Harbaugh overstates the psychological, personal component of clergy survival. For a pastor— for any Christian—"self-awareness" involves the realization that we are baptized, upheld, called, and held accountable to God in Jesus Christ. (Harbaugh says that "personhood" means "a person in Christ" [*Pastor as Person*].) I contend that this theological self-awareness is our most powerful resource for surviving and thriving in ministry. (Harbaugh devotes much attention in his work to spiritual development among pastors.) The root issue may not be the psychological one of finding people to support us in our struggles or of gaining enough ego strength to take care of "number one," but rather the theological problem of finding meaning in what we do in ministry.

Christians get their meaning and measure, the significance of what they do, from the church's book, the Bible. This story teaches us the peculiar point of view of the faithful community. How is our service in ministry, lay or pastoral, viewed from a biblical perspective? An illuminating episode is found in the Gospel of Luke. One day, the disciples said to Jesus, "Increase our faith" (Luke 17:7-10). In response, Jesus told them a story.

> Will any of you, who has a servant plowing or keeping sheep, say to him when he has come in from the field, "Come at once and sit down at table"? Will he not rather say to him, "Prepare supper for me and gird yourself and serve me, till I eat and drink; and afterward you shall eat and drink"? Does he thank the servant because he did what was commanded? So you also, when you have done all that is commanded you, say, "We are unworthy servants; we have only done what was our duty."

This story of the faithful servants is preceded by Jesus' admonition to "Beware of stumbling blocks to faith" (Luke 17:1). Evidently, a chief stumbling block is the expectation that our ministry will somehow be affirmed and confirmed by its recipients. While the desire for affirmation is a basic human need, a need to which the church ought to respond with greater sensitivity, the story suggests that it is of the nature of Christian ministry that affirmation is often in short supply.

On another occasion, someone says to Jesus that he
will follow him wherever he goes, but first "Let me first
go and bury my father." *Honor thy father and thy mother:*
it's one of the commandments. Jesus responds, "Leave
the dead to bury their own dead . . . go and proclaim
the kingdom of God" (Luke 9:60). Those are tough
words indeed.

What are we to make of a parable that characterizes
our response to Jesus' call in terms of *duty? Duty* has
become a dirty little word in modern parlance. *Duty* has
a gray, dogged, ugly sound, cousin to similarly
uninspiring words, such as *dullness, drudgery, discipline,*
and *determination. Duty*—it's not far in sound from an
even uglier Greek word, *doulos,* "slave," which the
Revised Standard Version of the Bible politely renders
"servant" in this text. *Doulos*—drudgery, duty.

Duty, once honored by Victorian moralists and
poets, has fallen on hard times and has been rendered
backseat status in ethical discourse. Duty, contemporary ethicists agree, is an inferior moral motivation.
What ought I do in the matter of an unwanted
pregnancy, selective service, Apartheid, marriage, and
ministry? Do your duty. When was the last time you
heard that urged? Today the main moral energies are
sensitivity, spontaneity, doing what comes naturally,
independent courage, or a careful, rational weighing of
the facts. *Duty* connotes blind obedience, mindless
reaction, the invidious Protestant work ethic, and
behavior that is little more than habit rather than heroic
choice and decision. The quaint young man who
proposed marriage to his pregnant girlfriend because

"It was my duty" has become the ethical equivalent of the whooping crane.

The venerable Augustine, when he struggled with this parable on servants and their duty, wondered if it could have come from the lips of the same Jesus who unabashedly rewarded the faithful steward (Luke 12:42-46) and promised a healthy return for those servants who invested their talents wisely (Luke 19:12-27).

In our world of the forty-hour week, this parable of the dutiful servants seems patently unfair. Surely the servant deserves a little appreciation, some expression of the Master's gratitude. But no, we are unworthy servants (or more accurately translated, worthless, miserable slaves) who have only done our duty.

Joachim Jeremias says that here is "an expression of modesty" (*The Parables of Jesus*, [New York: Charles Scribner's Sons, 1962], p. 193). No, Jesus is not talking about transforming unworthiness into a virtue or extolling the values of humility. Rather, duty is the key. Servants are those who owe the Master a sense of duty. Servants are in service to the Master.

Jesus' parable contains a definition of duty unlike that of the philosophers. Philosophy generally defines duty as that which one is morally obliged to do as opposed to what one may be pleased or inclined to do. For Aristotle, duty was ultimately pleasurable because it had as its end the achievement of our highest good, *eudaemonia*. The Stoics elevated duty as a supreme virtue. Stoic duty meant being true to oneself, acting as you are created to be. Kant made duty the very hallmark of morality. Kantian duty is the logical

90

response to the categorical imperative, that compelling action which is universally fitting.

As attractive as these accounts of duty may be, let us be clear that they have little to do with the duty of Jesus' parable. Here, duty is a response, not to whom we are (Stoics) or to whom most people ought to be (Kant) but to whom the Master is. Duty arises not from self-interest or even from kind concern for the self-interests of others, but rather out of a relationship between servant and Master.

In saying that we are unworthy servants who have only done our duty, the slaves are not feigning humility. They are stating what is true. They are indeed in service to the Master. Humility comes as a by-product of finding our lives and our projects caught up in something and someone greater than ourselves.

The parable suggests that the source of renewal and rejuvenation in ministry—a major defense against burnout in ministry, lay or pastoral—is renewed attentiveness to the Master, who calls each of us into service. The tough work of Christian ministry is the constant, daily, increasing challenge to take Jesus a little more seriously and ourselves a little less so. Against all definitions of ministry as a "profession" (as if some were professionals at it and others were amateurs), against all images of pastors as purveyors of certain esoteric skills to a lowly lay clientele, Jesus hurls this little story. All of our techniques, means of affirmation and support, skills, and understandings are only means of being more dutiful servants. Service does not primarily consist of various skills but of obedience. We must relearn the scandal of the New Testament:

Christian leaders being *diakanoi* (butler, waiter, servant) and of Paul saying that his only boasting lay in his pride at being a good slave for Christ.

The significance of the servant is incomprehensible apart from the projects and desires of the Master. The Master defines the shape of and validates the significance of faithful service. So our *diakonia* is integrally related to *leiturgia*. Times for prayer, meditation, and study are linked to our ability to minister, not because such times of reflection offer us the opportunity merely to delve deeper into our own egos (unworthy servants as we are) but because such times offer us the occasion to see more clearly the Master. As Augustine said, we imitate those whom we adore. So one of the toughest tasks of ministry is the job of making oneself more attentive, more adoring, of the One who modeled ministry with basin and towel, the One who came not to be served but to serve. "[Leadership] shall not be so among you" (Matt. 20:26), he said, as it was among the Gentiles.

There have been times in church history when the call to ministry was a call to crusade, to build, to fight. Now, in the mainline American Protestant church of our decade, it may be enough to hear a chastened, but equally challenging, call to duty.

People don't like to believe that their pastor visits them in the hospital, marries their young, buries their dead, listens to their troubles, and preaches the gospel out of something so mundane as duty. People may be shocked by the notion that someone teaches a third grade Sunday school class for twenty years because, "I felt that it was the least I could do for the Lord." Yet

92

more ministry is done for this reason than out of a desire for self-fulfillment.

Most pastors learn early on in ministry that if all you have is a vague desire to "help people" or to "discover the rewards of ministry," then you don't have much. What all of us need is something to keep us in ministry even when we don't feel like it, even when it doesn't please us to visit the sick, prepare our sermons, or teach the third grade Sunday school—even when no one affirms us or praises us. While I have often been critical of James D. Glasse's notion of the minister as a "professional" (*Profession: Minister: Confronting the Identity Crisis of the Parish Clergy* [Nashville: Abingdon], 1968) this image did have the virtue of reminding ministers that pastors are expected to give their best, despite their personal dilemmas or limitations at the moment. There are too many good reasons, having to do with the nature of human self-deception, and with the nature of the gospel, for us not to expect constant affirmation and support from the recipients of our ministry. In fact, the gospel teaches us to be uncomfortable particularly at those times when people tell us we are succeeding. Our main rationale for ministry, the primary source of our motivation, must be found elsewhere than in the praise or the blame of its recipients.

One of my former parishes had a rather extensive ministry to indigent, transient persons. Much of the time, I found it all rather annoying. The laypeople did their part, but because I was at the church more than anyone else, I often had to stop whatever I was doing and hand out food or clothing to someone who

93

professed a need and was passing through town. On one occasion, I was in my office late at night to study. I was startled by determined pounding on the front door of the church, the door I had carefully locked. Because it was a rather late hour, I thought I would ignore the pounding; the person might go away. But the pounding persisted. Much annoyed, I went down and opened the door to find, as I expected, a rather forlorn looking drifter who said he needed food and transportation out of town. I got the food and gave him enough money for a bus ticket.

He sullenly took what I gave him without a word of thanks. My vexation at his lack of acknowledgment of the church's generosity must have shown on my face because, as he was leaving, he turned and said, "I reckon that you expect me to fall down at your knees and say thanks because you have given me a sandwich and ten dollars." There was more than a hint of hostility in his voice. "Well, I won't. Your Jesus told you to give a cup of cold water and give to anybody who asks you, so you're *supposed* to do this for me."

I was furious as he slammed the door behind himself. Then it hit me. He was right. To put it all quite simply, Jesus did it and told us to do it and, therefore, it's our duty. The drifter had it right. Any alleged feelings of charity or pity or self-serving desires for his humble gratitude were quite beside the point. It is our duty. We owe it to our Master.

Robert Wilson and I did a study of small membership churches in North Carolina. We found that, for most pastors in the small membership church, ministry is no picnic. Most of the clergy we interviewed were demoralized, depressed, and disillusioned. But occasionally we found a pastor, nestled in some out of the way North Carolina crossroads, who could tell us in all sincerity that he or she really loved being a pastor of that little church. We probably ought to be more interested in those who do not burn out and who manage to keep at ministry rather than an exclusive focus on those who do. What made these pastors different?

"No ambition," was the answer we got from one church bureaucrat. "That's why they don't mind being stuck here."

We were drawn to a different conclusion. We decided that if you are a pastor who looks to the system for your affirmation, or who needs the approval and admiration of your peers to validate what you are doing in the church, then you are doomed to misery in a small membership church. Such churches cannot deliver those strokes. (Is it not risky to ask our ministry in any church to be validated by peers or the larger ecclesiastical system?) The happiest pastors seemed to be those who looked for affirmation from other sources. They were people who managed continually to be fascinated with the tasks of ministry. They loved to preach, liked nothing better than taking a text and working with it; whether they preached it to fifteen people or to five hundred made no difference to them. Their joy arose from their confidence that the task was intrinsically worthwhile.

Bultmann says of this parable of the faithful servant, "Jesus promises rewards to those who are obedient without thought of rewards" (*New Testament Theology*).

Paul could say to his small membership church, "I didn't preach myself to you but Jesus Christ as Lord. That's why I boast."

Every minister, clerical or lay, is tempted to abandon the task of service to the Master who is the Way, the Truth, and the Life, and make do with simply being popular or effective as the world measures such things. We must be careful not to respond to the phenomenon of burnout and dissipation of commitment in sub-Christian ways. Our ministry must be not only persistent and productive but also *faithful*. Ministry is, therefore, either based on our conviction that God really is present in the church—in word and sacrament, creating a new people who are capable of witnessing to God's kingdom—or ministry is misery. No amount of therapy or empathetic systems of support can help people who are not called to service. You can't pay people to do what ministers must do, and no amount of psychological self-esteem building can give us enough to keep at ministry when we no longer believe in it. In the end, our service is validated not by whether we find it particularly fulfilling (often we don't) or by whether the world finds it useful (usually it doesn't), but rather because what we do or say in service to Jesus Christ is true. We pastors serve God by serving a people who need no other service from us than to have their lives constantly directed to the living God. Failing at that, the temptation is to work for adjustment to the *status quo* or mere congregational conviviality where the minister becomes little more than a pop psychologist or the recreational director of the "love boat."

A kind of atheism is at the root of many ministerial

models today. This is an implicit assumption that God really doesn't matter as we go about building bigger and more active churches (church administration), developing self-esteem in our congregations (worship), helping discontented individuals adjust to their circumstances (pastoral counseling), enabling troubled souls to justify their basic self-centeredness (ethics), and offering Jesus as a worthy subject for poetic reflection (preaching). We go about assuming that it is up to us to make the kingdom of God happen. It's all on our shoulders. When we are faced with troubled people, we are told to "share" ourselves, to practice the "ministry of presence," as if we had it within our powers alone to heal them. When Henri Nouwen's "wounded healer" image of pastoral ministry (See *The Wounded Healer: Ministry in Contemporary Society* [New York: Doubleday, 1972]) is taken too far, it is apt to create a terrible confusion between our attributes as persons and the gifts we bear as pastors. Thank God that we have more to offer troubled souls than ourselves and our wounds. Pastors, without God, must work day and night, trying this and that and urging their laity to do the same, convinced that all that is needed is a little better preaching, a bit more dedication, or deeper personal empathy to bring the kingdom in on their terms. After all, if they don't do it, who will? Is it any wonder that clergy now report that they are suffering from burnout?

We are the servants of the Messiah, not the messiahs. We may preach justification by grace alone, but do we model this fundamental doctrine in our ministry? Do we pastors act as though everyone in the church but us is justified by the grace of God? When we alone determine the boundaries, goals, and mission of the church, who is to blame but us when our expectations are not fulfilled? By substituting utilitarian, socially approved concepts of ministry for the gospel's scandalous insistence that our ministry is but a reflection of God's activity in the world, we forfeit our means of dealing with the inevitable tragedy and failure that faithful ministry always entails.

Can we trust the Master to use our unworthy efforts in the service of what the Master desires? If we pastors want to help our people, this parable suggests that one of the most helpful things we can do is to give them something worth doing for someone who is worthy.

Some of the happiest, most committed people I know are artists. For example, the organist for my church will replay some phrase from a fugue until I, in my office trying to work on a sermon, am driven to near madness. When I complain about the excessive rehearsing, she replies, "You can empathize with me, preacher. You know what it's like to go over a sentence again and again until you get it right. The music demands and deserves it."

I remember my shock when, as an undergraduate student, I asked a famous writer, "How do you get yourself in the mood to write?"

She said, "I eat breakfast. I sit down at the typewriter and I write. I am a writer."

One time John Wesley complained to Peter Bohler that he was afraid he was loosing his faith—the eighteenth-century equivalent of burnout. "Go preach faith until you have it," was Bohler's no-nonsense exhortation to duty.

I would like always to feel loving, to be invigorated by the tasks of ministry, to be challenged by my people, to be loved and affirmed by my board. Unworthy as I am, I am not. But I can at least hope to be absorbed by something or someone greater than my feelings. I at least try to do my duty. And on most days, by the grace of God, it is enough.

IV

APPROPRIATE EVALUATION OF OUR MINISTRY

Anyone who burns out, drops out, or fades out of the church must have asked, at some point, either explicitly or subconsciously, "Should I stick with it?" Presumably, the person has answered that question in the negative. Something hasn't measured up. Either the church has not measured up to that person's expectations, or the person feels that he or she has not measured up to the church's expectations.

To answer the question "Should I stick with it?" some form of measurement, some means of evaluation, is required. The question cannot be answered without some definition of what ministry is, what the church is called to do, what God expects of us. In the preceding chapter of this book we have suggested, using one of Jesus' parables, that we ought to be ready for change in our conventional expectations when attempting definitions of the church and its ministry. Our definitions arise from scripture, which may present us with thoroughly counter-cultural, socially unacceptable, peculiar definitions of what is good, worthwhile, and

100

worth doing. Our Savior ended his earthly ministry on a cross, raised over a garbage dump. That is a peculiar image of salvation, to be sure.

There are, in the light of the gospel, good reasons for giving up on the church, good reasons for moving from one area of Christian service to another, appropriate times to call it quits and move on. The trick is to call it quits for the right reasons, to be sure that we have defined success or failure in terms that are congruent with the gospel rather than by whatever worldly standards may be closest at hand. To that end, let us conclude our exploration of burnout and dissipation in ministry by further biblical reflection on the peculiar nature of Christian ministry. If we burn out, drop out, or fade out, let it be because we have done so in service to the gospel rather than simply because we have misunderstood the gospel.

Success in Ministry: Life Among the Little Ones

A Vignette

The last book I read on my way out of seminary was Lyle Schaller's *The Change Agent*. That *was* to be me. But there I found myself, holding a wrench for Joe, lying on my stomach under an old lady's house. I am here holding the wrench because Joe is trying to fix a broken pipe, and he needed me. Joe is here because the night before I told Myrtle Jones, president of the Seekers Sunday School about the pipe under Mrs. Tallon's house. Myrtle had been working on Joe, trying to get him back to church after a mix up about the Bible study last year, so she thought that a good way to get at him would be to ask him to fix this leaking pipe. I was talking to Myrtle because, as president of the Seekers Class, she has been coordinating care for Mrs. Tallon since she slipped and broke her hip. Myrtle is the one who got into the fight with the hospital administrator downtown because he was trying to send Mrs. Tallon home before she was well. Myrtle got into it with the hospital administrator because her husband, Ted, when he was doing his hospital visitation duties, found Mrs. Tallon crying in her room because she had nowhere to go or no one to help her get by at home. Ted told her that the church would help and he knew lots of people who would bring by meals and sit with her until she got on her feet.

Myrtle demanded more time for the church to work out a solution. She had learned to fight at church, during her time as president of the United Methodist Women.

The hospital administrator gave in after the first round. Ted signed up a little boy to read to Mrs. Tallon on Thursdays, and that is when the water was discovered to be running somewhere under the house. The boy called the pastor because he didn't know what else to do, and that's why I was lying on my stomach under that house when I really ought to have been out changing the world. Some change agent!

Time and again, in interviews with pastors and those who attempt to help them, the grinding triviality of the church was mentioned. Our culture values success, progress, numerical growth, and change. We must admit that the majority of us mainline Protestant pastors will spend most of our ministry in situations where the size and the programs of the congregation either stay the same or become smaller.

Steven Sill, a Christian Church pastor, describes the guilt he felt as a pastor of a declining inner city congregation. His church "had been declining in membership for more than a decade. I felt that I must reverse this trend or I would fail as a minister. For every new family entering the fellowship, another moved away. We telephoned, we prayed, we worked, but saw few results. Sometimes I thought of leaving the ministry" ("Guilt or Grace?" *The Christian Ministry* (Nov.–Dec. 1987):6-7.) Small, declining churches with small, declining people—for many of us, this is Christian ministry.

So much of the pastoral ministry is consumed by petty, inconsequential, ordinary, little things—like an elderly woman's leaking pipes. Oh, to be done with this smallness and on to more important matters! Is it any wonder that many people, clergy and lay, give up on the church and drop out, engulfed as we are by such insignificance? Joe and me under Mrs. Tallon's house is not exactly changing the world.

Luke opens the story of Jesus' life with talk of insignificant things—such as old men, poor people, unmarried women, old childless women, and babies. He does so as if to turn out gaze from the great to the small, to warn us that we are about to hear a strange story that we might miss if we are unattentive to the little things.

> They were bringing even infants to him that he might touch them; and when the disciples saw it, they rebuked them. But Jesus called them to him, saying,

"Let the children come to me, and do not hinder them; for to such belongs the kingdom of God. Truly, I say to you, whoever does not receive the kingdom of God like a child shall not enter it." (Luke 18:15-17)

To hear this text about children we must see children for what they are, what they were in Jesus' day—dependent, nonproductive, demanding, frequently difficult intruders into our grown-up world. In Jesus' day, children were significant only as the Near Eastern equivalent to our Social Security system. If they lived past infancy, as few did, they were of some help in the never-ending task of securing food for the family. They were, in other words, at the bottom of society.

The adults were listening to Jesus one day. Everybody was taking notes. Everybody was trying to listen carefully, to get it right. And they said to Jesus, "Can't something be done about these children? They're distracting. Send them to children's church or something."

But Jesus said, "Let them come . . . this is the kingdom." This is a kingdom in which the door is small. You can't get in unless you are a child, unless you are little.

Of course, that's bad news. Who, especially in our world, wants to be little, vulnerable, weak, small, dependent? Yet, Jesus says that *this* is the kingdom.

Jesus begins a sermon by saying: "Blessed are you poor; blessed are you hungry." Blessed are you unemployed. Oh, how lucky are those of you going through marital distress. Oh, how fortunate are you with a terminal illness. The congregation does a double-take. Fortunate? Lucky? In this country, when

104

you are unemployed, people treat you as if you were diseased. They are afraid that whatever you have might be catching. They avoid you. They tell you that if you played by the rules, you wouldn't be unemployed. Jesus says, "Excuse me. I'm sorry. I wasn't talking about the American Way, I was talking about God's kingdom, where the first shall be last and the last first."

My point about these little ones is that one of the principal tasks of the pastor is to hold up to the congregation, by word and deed, our peculiar Christian vision of what the world really is—namely, a place where Jesus is present in the "least of these." All of us are called to that ministry by virtue of our baptism, according to I Peter. The church has priests in order to illuminate (not eliminate) the priest in all of us.

We have a problem because many of our people have come to associate being faithful Christians with being ordained to the priesthood. As we noted earlier, the term *lay ministry* has come to mean merely assisting the clergy in their ministry, which usually means helping the institutional church to keep clunking along.

The ordained ministry arose when the early church realized that it was going to be given another day to live. Persons were chosen from the church to preside over its gatherings so that it could remember and represent the story and thereby be empowered for ministry. The community gave these persons authority to work for the good of the community because they demonstrated particular gifts and graces for building up the church.

These priestly duties included assembling the church, proclaiming the word, and giving guidance to the congregation in its mission and service. But the early church never intended for these functions to be carried on in an exclusive manner. Everyone participated in their fulfillment. Whenever an ordained person preached, it was in a representative way to provide unity and continuity for the whole church. *All* baptized persons are in ministry. Those Christians who are called by the church to ordination will find their primary ministry within the church. The ministry of the laity is within the world. The primary mission of the church lies outside the church, but priests and pastors function primarily within the church so that the laity may be about their ministry in the world.

Many of us priests in mainline, liberal Protestantism have become diverted from our central focus: the building up of the congregation. Rather than do what we were ordained to do—namely, care for the congregation—we began improving the world. We bought into the imperialistic assumption that someone had ordained us to look after the whole town rather than to equip the people of God. No wonder our pastors grew empty and tired. We assumed that since America was at least a vestigially Christian country, we didn't have to worry about forming a visible people of God. We could go out and do politics, lobby the school board, and things would take care of themselves at the church. We underestimated how very difficult it is, even in God-we-trust America (perhaps *especially* here), to create a community of truth, a community willing to see little ones for who they really are and the big, powerful ones for who they really are. The most politically significant thing the church can do is to be the church, and the most politically helpful thing pastors can do is to help form the church—a people who are formed by listening to the peculiar story, which is scripture.

Jesus lays a most peculiar vision of community upon us. Only constant attentiveness, weekly reiteration, and every-Sunday rehearsal will keep this vision before us. We become so distracted with talk of empowerment, liberation, and fulfillment that we can't see what is real.

They were listening to Jesus one day, everybody trying hard to pay attention, everyone taking notes, everyone trying to get the point—and when you're somebody like Simon Peter, that isn't easy! So they said to Jesus, "Send these little ones, these children away so that we can pay attention."

Remember what Jesus did. He pulled a child out of the crowd and put the child in the middle of them saying, "When you receive one such child in my name, you receive me."

He put the child there to help them pay attention.

Like the gospel itself, church happens in small, unspectacular ways—a plumber and a preacher fixing somebody's pipes. This is ministry, receiving little ones in the name of the One who blessed little ones. Do we fully realize how revolutionary, how countercultural a thing it is in our society for someone, without pay in the name of Christ, to spend an afternoon visiting a eighty-year-old shut-in?

"People leave the ministry," one counselor told me, "because they drown in the trivialities of the church. They knock their brains out for some little church somewhere and, about ten or twenty years into it, step back and ask themselves, 'What does it all mean? What good have I done?' That's when they call it quits."

I can understand that. It is well to ask of our ministry what difference it makes. What good have we done? But we must ask such questions always in the proper context, against the backdrop of this strange good news, which has a tendency to measure fidelity with a peculiar yardstick. Jesus wept over his failure to win Jerusalem, and he grew angry at the perversion of his beloved temple. He was repeatedly frustrated by the inability of his disciples to hear and to act on his teaching. "What am I to do with you?" he asked on one occasion. "You are like children!"

But his ministry was always measured by its relationship to the "little ones"—the poor, the sick, the maimed, the lame, and the blind. He spent his life among those whom the world regarded to be of no account. When it was over, the world could walk by his cross and say, "What a waste," for the world knew not the nature of his good news. It all seemed so terribly insignificant.

Pastor Sill decided that, if he were to serve faithfully in his inner city church,

> I must free myself of the secular world's preoccupation with success. I had begun feeling like a beleaguered football coach facing ouster because his team had won only two games all season. I began to see that in their interactions, pastors mirrored society's competitiveness. Only, rather than asking questions like, "What kind of car are you driving?" they asked, "Where are you serving now?" or "How many are you running in Sunday School?" They boasted, "Our new building is

nearly finished!" But in a competitive system no one wins all the time, and feelings of failure and guilt go hand in hand ("Guilt or Grace?" p. 6).

As a pastor, I wish that I had a greater ability to do for my people what Jesus did that day for his disciples: point to ministry when it happens in seemingly small and insignificant ways in my congregation. I believe that I would do a better job of building up the visible body of Christ if I were better able to say, "Hey, everybody, look over here. You want to be a minister? Come, look! You don't get to see the gospel too often in this place. Everybody, come look."

Can we trust God to provide the results that God desires? Is our ministry so bold, countercultural, and visionary that it will fail miserably without the grace of God? Sill looks ahead to the time when his ministry will be ultimately evaluated.

> When I meet my Lord I think he will ask, "Have you been faithful?" but certainly not "How many people did you add to your churches' membership rolls?" I am, finally, dependent upon God's grace. His love and not my competitive efforts will produce the lasting results. It is my part to "preach the word, being urgent in season and out of season" (I Timothy 4:2). But I must be content with the results God provides ("Guilt or Grace?" p. 7).

So why am I still here? For the same reason as you: holding the wrench for Joe, so that he can be a minister in the name of the one who said, "Whenever you receive one such child in my name, you receive me."

CONCLUSION:

MOSES' MINISTRY AND OUR OWN

On Sunday, after I've finished preaching in Duke Chapel and have retreated to my appointed perch—the seat behind the alto section, where the preacher blends into the woodwork—I often look up, during the offering, to the stained-glass window high above and across from where I sit. As preacher, I sit across from the Moses window. Hardly anyone else in the Chapel can see this window. Surrounding a stark, towering Moses is a collection of scenes from his life: Moses raised by royalty; Moses the angry defender of the oppressed; Moses the liberator, the lawgiver; Moses who leads Israel out of bondage to the Promised Land.

Somehow, at about 11:45 on Sunday morning, when I've finished preaching and am sitting there behind the altos, the sun highlights one Moses scene more than the rest. It's the last scene in his ministry: Moses held back from entering the Promised Land. Yahweh let Moses get to the door, but would not allow him to go over the threshold with Israel. Whether the creator of that stained-glass window intended to force the preacher to ponder that scene week in and week out, I am not sure. But it works. When I look at the end of Moses' ministry, I am reminded of my own.

There is much unfulfillment in the church. A great deal of life is spent on the verge, at the door, but not over the threshold. We must, like Moses, be content with sowing and leave the harvest for others. The choir sings, I preach, and God only knows where it all leads, what land of promise will be opened through our ministry. God only knows.

> And let us not grow weary in well-doing, for in due season we shall reap, if we do not lose heart. So then, as we have opportunity, let us do good to all . . . and especially to those who are of the household of faith. (Galatians 6:9-10)

We began this exploration of burnout, dropout, and faith dissipation in ministry with Moses, seeing his ministry as a kind of paradigm of our own. Now let us allow the end of Moses' ministry to remind us that if we are going to keep at Christian ministry as preachers, altos, or to whatever service God calls us, we will do so only by having the confidence that God really does convey treasure through our earthen vessel. God really does put us to good purposes, even though we may not see them clearly and even though we may not enter the Promised Land of concrete results and visible fulfillment with those whom we have tried to uphold in the exodus from here to there.